The myth of good AI

Manchester University Press

FUTURES

AI *Futures* presents a critical analysis of Artificial Intelligence with a particular emphasis on its implication for society. It connects research into the ethics of AI to research initiatives focused on the variegated impacts of Artificial Intelligence, including on marginalised communities and on the Global South. As such, *AI Futures* encompasses a unique range of studies into the political, socio-economic, medical, biological and environmental questions raised by the onset of this new age in global history.

Series Editor

Professor Arshin Adib-Moghaddam, SOAS, University of London

Editorial Board

Aldo Alvarez-Risco, Associate Professor of International Business, University of Lima

Tugrul Keskin, Professor of Global Studies and Director of the Centre for Global Governance, Shanghai University

Bogna Konior, Assistant Professor of Media Theory, Interactive Media Arts Department, New York University, Shanghai

Nandita Biswas Mellamphy, Associate Professor of Political Theory, University of Western Ontario

Jason Mohaghegh, Associate Professor of Comparative Literature and Philosophy, Babson College

To buy or to find out more about the books currently available in this series, please go to: https://manchesteruniversitypress.co.uk/series/ai-futures/

The myth of good AI

A manifesto for critical
Artificial Intelligence

Arshin Adib-Moghaddam

MANCHESTER UNIVERSITY PRESS

Copyright © Arshin Adib-Moghaddam 2025

The right of Arshin Adib-Moghaddam to be identified as the author of this work has been asserted in accordance with the Copyright, Designs and Patents Act 1988.

No AI technology was knowingly used in the process of researching and/or writing this book.

Published by Manchester University Press
Oxford Road, Manchester, M13 9PL
www.manchesteruniversitypress.co.uk

British Library Cataloguing-in-Publication Data
A catalogue record for this book is available from the British Library

ISBN 978 1 5261 8949 3 hardback
ISBN 978 1 5261 8950 9 paperback

First published 2025

The publisher has no responsibility for the persistence or accuracy of URLs for any external or third-party internet websites referred to in this book, and does not guarantee that any content on such websites is, or will remain, accurate or appropriate.

EU authorised representative for GPSR:
Easy Access System Europe, Mustamäe tee 50, 10621 Tallinn, Estonia
gpsr.requests@easproject.com

Typeset by Newgen Publishing UK

Contents

Introduction: The delirious society	1
1 Debugging machine ethics	22
2 Eugenic racism	53
3 Techno-Orientalism	76
4 The future of scientific torture	102
Conclusion: After AI	125
Select bibliography	150
Index	165

Introduction
The delirious society

'There is truth and there is untruth'. I am taking this phrase from a particularly compelling yet also discomforting section of the trailer for the movie of George Orwell's novel *1984*.[1] In what is probably the most famous depiction of a dystopian future – written in the best tradition of British anti-totalitarian thought – where free thinking is considered a thought-crime, there was still room for resistance precisely because the delineation between right and wrong was still visible, could still be grasped and used as a catalyst for emancipation. This is a good example of the certainty of a world from which we have departed.

The delirious society that we are living in resembles a perfectly staged untruth that we are persuaded to accept as reality. To understand how this untruth came about and how Artificial Intelligence worsens its outcomes for society is the topic of this book. The new techno-politics, driven by this insatiable infatuation with AI power marketed by companies such as X (Twitter), Google, Microsoft and Meta, is the mechanism through which that mirage of a reality is created in such a perfectly organised way that it blurs the lines of our traditional understandings of truth and untruth, power and resistance, subjectivity and objectivity, science and fiction. Big Brother is not only watching us from the outside any more. The present book will show how Big Brother is lodging himself deeply inside our cognitive faculties, almost like a microbe within the neurons of our frontal lobe, where our cognitive functions are processed. This is why I call this first of our concepts for understanding the delirious society *psycho-codification*.

Orwell cannot help us, and nor can the famous post-structuralist French philosopher Michel Foucault, one of the greatest minds of the twentieth century. What he called biopower was already intrusive, as Foucault conceptualised power as a gliding phenomenon that is omnipresent; power as a projectile that would discipline and govern our bodies in an immensely flexible and sophisticated manner.[2] But even Foucault's biopolitics was naive, too hinged upon the benign forms of governmentality in the latter half of the twentieth century. The panopticon – that famous architectural construct developed by the British social reformer Jeremy Bentham at the end of the eighteenth century as the 'modern prison' – does not begin to explain the immensely minute control that Artificial Intelligence exerts upon us.[3] Foucault used the panopticon as a metaphor to explain how the modern individual was 'reformed' into a disciplined yes-sayer. By assuming that we are constantly watched, (European) modernity ordered away our human complexities in favour of a docile mentality and utilitarian lifestyle. This is our social reality at the moment. To grasp that battle with a digitally induced, delirious unfreedom is the first step towards reclaiming our individuality, autonomy and agency as democratic citizens. Yes, it is freedom that is at stake, even if this may sound too preposterous a statement at this early stage of the present book.

Introduction: The delirious society

Today, the assault on our autonomy is massive. The panopticon, the modern prison, has been turned into something even more intrusive, even in advanced democracies. The Torre Centilena (Sentinel Tower) in Ciudad Juárez, Mexico is a good example. It serves as a scary analogy for our surveilled lives. The surveillance tower is being equipped with 1791 licence plate readers, at least 74 drones and 3,065 pan-tilt zoom cameras. All of that techno-gaze is forensically focused on every individual in the area through connections to 'smart city' applications which are also supplied with biometric filters running constantly to identify individuals via AI-powered facial recognition software. At a cost of US$200 million, the Sentinel Tower has twenty storeys and is meant to police the border between Mexico and the United States.[4]

Elsewhere in Latin America, the right-wing president of Argentina, Javier Milei, created an 'Artificial Intelligence Applied to Security Unit' as a part of the Argentinian *Ministerio de Seguridad*. The legislation sets out that the unit will employ 'machine learning algorithms to analyse historical crime data to predict future crimes'.[5] Wanted persons would be identified through facial recognition software. In addition, real-time security footage is already used to detect potential crimes. Finally, social media sites would be patrolled to monitor online activity. The incredibly resourceful civil society organisations in Argentina immediately interjected that such technologies have been used to suppress political dissent from the oppositional media, academics and activists and that the AI unit seriously threatens the privacy of Argentinian citizens. According to a post on X from the Argentine Centre for Studies on Freedom of Expression and Access to Information, the 'opacity in the acquisition and implementation of such technologies and the

The myth of good AI

lack of accountability are worrying'.[6] Regarding such architectures of surveillance, the research underlying this book clearly demonstrates that the technological opportunities of today, and more exponentially in the future, deliver something that twentieth-century states and multinational companies could only dream of: The prospect of full micro-organismal psycho-codification of the individual which would allow for a recoding of subjectivity that is near-total.

Power is not only a gliding projectile with immense velocity any more. Power is becoming as digestible and penetrative as liquid. 'Be as water', the famous Chinese martial arts actor Bruce Lee once said: 'You must be shapeless, formless, like water. When you pour water in a cup, it becomes the cup. When you pour water in a bottle, it becomes the bottle. When you pour water in a teapot, it becomes the teapot. Water can drip and it can crash. Become like water my friend'.[7] In our case, power in a liquidised form takes the shape of whatever it enters and so it becomes almost invisible. This is a new form of bio-insecurity for humanity which threatens to turn us into Kinskian Nosferatus of the governing elites; undead canvases for that perfectly staged untruth, which we will accept as reality because we are being coded, from head to toe, to do so.

The delirious society and the individual entangled within it are the future of control on an unimaginable scale. Our near-total psycho-codification is accompanied by a surveillance regime that can only be characterised as microbial, exactly because it is aquatic, shapeless and formless, to use Bruce Lee's analogy. This *microbial surveillance* is our second concept for understanding our delirium in this age of Artificial Intelligence. As we are tiptoeing into a future where we will be walking around smart cities densely controlled by sensors,

Introduction: The delirious society

cameras and drones tracking our every movement, we will be total objects of power, certainly in the public sphere much in the same way as Steven Spielberg's movie *Minority Report* starring Tom Cruise and Colin Farrell postulated. As the research of Patricia Tapia, Aldo-Alvarez-Risco and Shyla Del-Aguila-Arcentales shows,[8] smart cities are the future – certainly also because they are aggressively marketed as sustainable by the 'good AI' proponents.[9]

In this regard, the future is already here and forging ahead with supersonic speed, threatening to leave you behind while you are reading these cautionary notes. My examples may already be outdated shortly after I have written these lines, superseded by ever more perfected forms of psycho-codification and microbial surveillance. But these examples are curated to illustrate the future by augmenting and scaling what is already happening. For instance, a so-called smart digital billboard in London's Piccadilly Circus equipped with in-built cameras uses responsive recognition technology to display targeted advertisements based on passing pedestrians' gender and age or the make of passing cars. In Hangzhou, a city of over eleven million people in the east of China, an AI-driven smart city system has been in place since 2016. It uses big data and machine learning to monitor every vehicle in the city. Other cities in China have installed facial recognition software that is linked to huge databases with private information, number plates, addresses, bank accounts etc.[10] If the panopticon would still allow for some dark corners where you could hide and express your subjectivity, the future smart city supervised by a sentinel tower makes it almost impossible for anyone to live freely in the shadows. Psycho-codification and microbial surveillance are merging and will continue until they deliver full control if we don't put the brakes on.

The myth of good AI

As we are quickly becoming avatars in a *SimCity*-like simulation, our every movement can be tracked by a combination of highly intrusive AI-driven technology. Such video-game-style visualisation could easily link to your social media profile, your family pictures stored in your cloud services and your Alexa at home perusing your shopping habits, listening to your voice and favourite music. Imagine a smart city HQ, where technocrats would sit and say: 'Oh, this is what he buys.', 'Oh, that's where his girlfriend lives.' and 'Interesting, so that's where he hides things.'

Furthermore, cyber-armies all over the world are already engaged in a global hacking competition aimed at various critical infrastructures. From the health-care sector, as the repeated attacks on the United Kingdom's National Health Service exemplify, and nuclear installations, for instance, the Stuxnet malware attack on Iran's nuclear energy facilities, these various forms of hybrid warfare can easily turn our AI-driven devices into weapons and sites on an ever-expanding battlefield with no bunker to hide in. In fact, at the time of writing, the Israeli military had remotely detonated walkie-talkies and pagers used by members of Lebanon's Hezbollah movement in the first instance of such killings in modern warfare. There is no precedent in human history for such immediacy of conflict.[11] The war can emerge from everywhere, as we are already using the 'iWeapons' that can be turned into bombs on an everyday basis.

Our everyday lives as avatars in a virtual reality are preprogrammed and mapped out on the neuronal pathways of electrodes that are lodged in our immediate social reality and absorbed by our frontal cortex. Doesn't this dialectic between AI-technology-driven systems and the individual demand a new philosophical approach that interrogates the realm of

Introduction: The delirious society

posthumanity? Doesn't it beget a new dimension of social angst as the lines between *Mensch* and robot are increasingly blurred? We are already becoming accustomed to talking to our digital assistants as if they are human. Some of us are starting to treat them as cyberfriends, even therapists and confidants. Data compiled by Google Trends in 2023 indicate a 2,400 per cent increase in searches for 'AI girlfriends'.[12] Virtual friends are increasingly embedded in smartphones and popular applications such as Snapchat which introduced 'My AI' in 2023. This is an 'AI companion' that adopts your preferences in accordance with your clicks in the app. And companies such as Romantic AI advertise 'the best girlfriend ever', which would be at 'your fingertips' in a true nightmare scenario for all feminists. 'Bots are hot and ready, *text now*!', the marketing banner exclaims.[13] These devices, programs, companies and their apps have clearly been created to be compliant; they lack the human intuition that can only develop through self-reflection. In this sterilised, narcissistic world where machines replace our social relationships and turn into mere objects of our devotion and desires, deep human connections are increasingly inhibited.[14]

The consequences of this posthumanity are not only social. As indicated, the more sinister impact of AI-driven technology will be on the battlefield, in that realm of human activity where questions of life and death are determined by split-second decisions. *Posthuman warfare* is our third concept. Already, civilians are routinely killed by military drones piloted by humans.[15] In the future we will face a mode of social and military warfare that compounds the problem of killing and torturing without accountability. Imagine swarms of quadcopter killer drones equipped with unconventional weapons (e.g. biological, chemical), which are only a very small technological advance away.

The myth of good AI

It is not only terrorists who could easily get their hands on such technology, and such AI-driven 'terror-bots' open up immensely challenging questions about ethics on the battlefield and within society. Our current legal system and certainly the Geneva Convention seem woefully outdated to deal with an army of *Ex-Machina*-style terminators that are programmed to kill and maim.[16]

Once these forms of new posthuman warfare are developed and deployed, they become factors in world politics, and not only for us, but also for homicidal movements that are summarised with the label 'terrorist'. How willing are the tech-giants – and how capable are governments – to stem their profits and power in order to institute an ethical code of conduct that would harmonise some of the battle lines that are already opening up between human and machine? For a rather more responsible approach to prevail, we need a global movement with local manifestations that makes the case for peaceful deployment of AI-driven technology. Where there is power, there is always resistance.[17] Making the case that AI technology is only progressive, even admissible, when it helps us in fighting poverty, famines, environmental degradation and war is a future task for all of us.[18] It may well be the cosmic battle of the next generations, and it will decide if human civilisation will survive as we know it.

AI angst

The present study delves into both our multiple predicaments and future antidotes to try to vaccinate us against the nauseating impact of this AI-induced delirium. To that end, we trace an attack on our senses by some of the AI technology out there

Introduction: The delirious society

and the bad data that flow into its algorithmic illogic. We have entered a period of social and political disorder, where truth and lies are no longer distinguishable. This is a world that is by far more sinister than even the most deprecated social and political systems in human history. As mentioned earlier, in Orwell's *1984* the locus of power and surveillance was visible. It was the totalitarian state, commonly referring to the Nazi party organised around Adolf Hitler that ruled Germany between 1933 and 1945. Another example would be the Soviet Union and its totalitarian Communist ideology, in particular in its Stalinist variant. Today, many commentators in Europe, Australia, New Zealand and North America like to point to North Korea, Putin's Russia or China as totalitarian polities.

But this is not the entirety of the delirious society that we have entered. The results of the research that informed this book are scarier by far. Our work exposes some of the nefarious effects of AI technology and the dangers for human security:[19] Facial recognition software that wrongly criminalises Black and Asian minorities leading to a string of wrongful arrests in the United States and elsewhere; recidivism software that clearly discriminates against Black offenders; tragically wrong healthcare decisions due to algorithms that are trained on 'White data'; denial of mortgages for minority populations facilitated by biased datasets and so on.

Repeatedly, AI technology has been indicted for being ageist, racist and misogynist. The present study is undergirded by primary materials gathered from all over the world that make this clear. Already, scholars and activists are starting to focus on the whole spectrum of AI discrimination. My research here and in *Is Artificial Intelligence Racist?*[20] bundles and conceptualises these joint efforts by highlighting what is going wrong and by putting forward ideas about what can be done to improve the situation. For example, there is a lot of fanfare about how AI promises to streamline health-care provision for the elderly. But there is an emerging sub-field that reveals severe forms of digital ageism. In a detailed review of the current state of the scholarship, colleagues rightly establish that digital 'exclusion can significantly impact older adults due to ageist stereotypes, for example, the development of select social media applications based on the perceived needs of older adults, as well as exclusion from clinical research which results in a lack of data about the effects of medications on older adults'. Quite comparably to other forms of algorithmic discrimination, 'digital ageism is deeply entangled with societal biases and wider structural inequalities. A concerted multifaceted interdisciplinary effort will be needed to begin to effectively address them.'[21]

So every aspect of our life is already governed by such oppressive algorithms. In many fields of society, AI is making matters worse, as it is sold to us as essentially unbiased, as 'good AI'.[22] Already, the most vulnerable are left behind, entrenching socio-economic hierarchies. For example, in the United States, it is estimated that 70 per cent of companies[23] – and 99 per cent of Fortune 500[24] companies – use AI to hire staff. McDonald's uses an AI chatbot on a platform called Paradox.ai to interview candidates about their work experience, address and the working hours that they expect. The system does a background check almost instantly and cuts the hiring process from a fortnight to about a couple of days.

Moreover, AI hiring tools increasingly rate personality traits to gauge the suitability of candidates for the job, and 'aggression detectors' tell the AI hiring bot about the 'stress resistance' of the candidate. As we will see along the way, all of this is

Introduction: The delirious society

based on bad legacies in our sciences that are perfectionist at best and eugenicist at worse. Imagine someone with a difference in the way they speak due to hearing loss, someone with a stammer, an accent or a speech impediment. The AI chatbot would rate them as poorly qualified for most customer-related jobs because of a 'lack of speaking ability'. Individuals whose vision is impaired, or those who are neurodivergent, may find it difficult to maintain eye contact, which could be interpreted by an AI-system as an inability to focus or concentrate.[25] As Maitreya Shah, a blind researcher at Harvard's Berkman Klein Center for Internet and Society, flags: 'A lot of research so far has focused on how AI technologies discriminate against people with disabilities, how algorithms harm people with disabilities.' On top of this, we need 'to talk about how even the conversation on AI fairness, which was purportedly commenced to fix AI systems and to mitigate harms, also does not adequately account for the rights, challenges, and lived experiences of people with disabilities'. The case Shah makes for inclusivity, an important ingredient of any critical AI manifesto, is crucial here:

> If you don't incorporate disability data, your algorithms would be open to discriminating against people with disabilities because they don't fit the normative ideas of your algorithms. If you incorporate the data, a lot of people with disabilities would still be missed out because inherently, the way you incorporate datasets, you divide data on the axes of identity. ... Let people with disabilities participate in the development and the deployment of technologies. Let them decide what is good for them, let them decide how they want to define or shape their own identities.[26]

We are told that machines don't lie and that they will deliver a better future for everyone. This pseudo-objectiveness is central

The myth of good AI

to the AI hype that has been created by the so-called tech-giants. It is easily discernible from the speeches of Elon Musk, Mark Zuckerberg and Bill Gates, even if now and then they warn us about the projects that they themselves are responsible for. On a more fundamental level, basic human rights are threatened, as legal accountability is blurred by the maze of technology placed between the perpetrators and the various forms of discrimination that can be conveniently blamed on the machine. The present book will dissect some of these dangerous trends, and it will interrogate the idea that AI can be ethical.

In fact, we can move one step further. The 'bad guys' in history have always used technology to propagate some ideas and suppress others. Adolf Hitler's propaganda minister Joseph Goebbels sponsored the *Volksempfänger*, a range of low-cost German radio receivers, to reach the living-rooms of German households and to agitate against Jewish people and other minorities and to advocate war. Today, the reach of technology is much more extensive, as our Alexas, Siris and smartphones govern almost every aspect of our life: From AI-powered toilets, to networked toys for children. The resurgent right wing in Europe and the United States celebrates as vile religious fundamentalists and extremists all over the world are sweetening their toxic brew in an AI candy shop that allows them unfettered access to all areas of society – a great propaganda feat that they could only have dreamt about even a decade ago. As a recent UNESCO report establishes:

> Generative AI must be trained using vast amounts of data. This data is often mined from the Internet and may include misleading or harmful content. AI systems therefore inherit human biases, potentially misrepresenting information about specific events,

Introduction: The delirious society

> reinforcing prejudices. This is particularly true in the context of [the] Holocaust, because of the prevalence [*sic*] disinformation about this event. ... Deepfake images and audio content created using Generative AI are particularly convincing for young people, who may encounter them on social media platforms. The Historical Figures App allowed users to chat with prominent Nazis such as Adolf Hitler and Joseph Goebbels, and falsely claimed that individuals such as Goebbels were not intentionally involved in the Holocaust and had tried to prevent violence against Jews.[27]

By logging on to the Internet of Things (IoT), we connect to a scary world. Criminal gangs use AI algorithms to pinpoint vulnerable families and the elderly. The newest AI applications allow scammers to simulate being a relative, often a grandchild, who claims to be in trouble and requires money to bail him/herself out. Digital voice apps can realistically imitate anyone's speech based on voice samples gathered online. ChatGPT would be used to transform all of this into a dialogue with authentic questions and answers. Video apps are progressing very quickly, too. Already, you may be faced by a fake Zoom call from a computer-generated relative invented by a scammer who can't be located due to his VPN-shielded IP address.

The vulnerable strata of society are the most convenient targets. For instance, the National Crime Agency (NCA) of the United Kingdom recently forecast that AI could worsen the abuse of children.[28] On the one hand, AI applications make it that much easier for abusers to hide their identity, shielding them from persecution. On the other hand, the use of AI for sexual exploitation will make it harder to identify real children who need to be protected as opposed to fake ones that are created with increasingly sophisticated image-generating applications.

The myth of good AI

The NCA report indicates the endless opportunities offered by such AI tools. Apparently, they are already celebrated by abusers on their illegal online chat forums.[29]

Social media channels are used to organise people trafficking, sell drugs, teach people how to build bombs, buy weapons and commit suicide, to kill, maim and smuggle. In our delirious society, where it is difficult to disentangle the truth/reality from the untruth, our private space isn't legally protected because our personal data is the fuel that keeps the tech-giants going. The right to privacy and the concomitant ownership of our virtual and real-life data are not codified as a human right, allowing the data to be harvested as a means to create ever more sophisticated data that spur the AI machines into action.

Delirium is about hallucinations that are meant to scare us. The delirious society is intended to instil fear, one of the central emotions that make us human and therefore more vulnerable than the AI machine. Fear is innate, part of our genetic DNA. On the most basic level, our fight-or-flight instinct, which is triggered by a sense of danger, is the reason why we humans have survived as a species. Also known as the acute stress response, we inherited the fight-or-flight response from our forebears, whose fearful environment triggered a life-saving physiological reaction driven by adrenaline that prepares our body to either stay and deal with a threat or to run away to safety. It is that discomforting feeling we get in our stomach when we are nervous due to a particularly stressful situation. This type of response has a productive, life-saving effect that has been crucial to our existence. Ultimately, there is nothing wrong with being afraid of a situation, if you can manage the response. In fact, your body is designed to turn you into a better-performing person when you are terrified.

Introduction: The delirious society

But fear can also be debilitating to mind and body. This is the case when you are living under conditions where there is constant stress, an unending absence of certainty and continuous invasion of your privacy, even of your inner self. The delirious society is like supersonic bursts of tinnitus that we can't anticipate. But it is coded in a way that regulates stress to a constant level of acceptance, never quite triggering our natural fight-or-flight response. The point I am trying to make is that the fight-or-flight response primes us to be better-performing individuals when we are faced with acute stress, meaning it happens suddenly and sporadically. However, in the delirious society, and certainly in the future that Artificial Intelligence is delivering for us, fear is provoked systematically as it emanates from different loci. If only it was just your commute or boss causing you stress. No, we are living in a system that is loaded with stress factors that are structural, long-term and tightly woven into our daily lives and cognition. In short, we are made to be afraid, as inducing angst is a system of governance. It is this function of fear as governance that I will dissect in this book, as Artificial Intelligence enhances the ability of conglomerates to terrify us whenever necessary for the purposes of control, surveillance and ultimately profit.

In this effort to confront the untruth of AI algorithms with critical, life-affirming and humane concepts steeped in 'global thought' – that is ideas that speak to our universally shared human sentiments – the present study connects with recent strides towards what I started to conceptualise as 'critical AI studies' in my previous book on the subject, which serves as a prequel to the present study.[30] Young scholars such as Abeba Birhane occupy a similarly critical space, shifting the discussion towards the harmful effects of machines.[31] Scholar-activists such as Joy Buolamwini, who has founded the Algorithmic Justice League, use various forms of digital art to engage the machines and their algorithms on their turf.[32] Some of these critical interventions can be easily connected to counter-cultural ideas of the 1960s and 1970s, expressed all over the world, for instance, to the emphasis on coloniality in the writings of Peru's Aníbal Quijano or to the work of Iran's Jalal Al-e Ahmad, especially to his irresistible assault on the dehumanising effects of 'the machine', the 'westtoxification' (*Gharbzadegi*) of those 'oppressed' by western modernity. As Hamid Dabashi, one of the few cross-cultural and transnational thinkers of our current era observes:

> Between the 1960s and the 1990s groundbreaking work was done in Latin America to expand our critical encounter with European coloniality. Al-e Ahmad himself and his nativist critics were entirely oblivious to this project. But, and there is the crucial point, Al-e Ahmad's *Gharbzadegi* shared the same critical consciousness of alerting the world that one soul at least in Iran was thinking the same way.[33]

Some of this beautifully aesthetic criticism is mirrored in the must-read writings of Herbert Marcuse and his indictment of 'one-dimensional man', who has lost the ability to think freely. This doyen of the counter-culture of the 1960s and 1970s agitated from various global settings. Marcuse and his 'Frankfurt School' had a lot to say about the future that is our present. Knowing about and studying them is crucial to confront the techno-power dominating our age of AI and to equip ourselves with a survival kit to be able to live our lives free of the perils of psycho-codification, microbial surveillance and posthuman warfare. In fact, to build ourselves our own library of critical knowledge – a refuge from the delirious society and its digital

Introduction: The delirious society

tinnitus effect – is the best prophylaxis to enable our survival. In that space we can read and reflect, think and act. We need that library in every private space. We need to study it. We need the books to safeguard culture. Therefore, the emancipative ideas of critical theorists will accompany us throughout this study, and they should do so in our everyday life.[34]

With these goals in mind, chapter 1 reframes some of the problematic notions underlying current advances in machine ethics using a philosophical approach that is informed by global knowledge, while at the same time furthering the case for 'critical AI studies'. Chapter 2 connects the historical legacies of European forms of colonial thinking and practices to a new geopolitics that AI entrenches. It also continues to experiment with ideas that are strong enough to produce better 'data' and therefore more humane outcomes from our AI machines. Chapter 3 continues this crucial discussion of the past and its implications for our algorithmic future, with a particular emphasis on processes of social marginalisation and political oppression that are largely ignored by the 'good AI' lobby. It also highlights the lack of engagement with the nefarious effect of AI technology, for instance, with regard to the horrors of contemporary torture techniques. Hence, chapter 4 looks at the ways in which technology poses a threat to human security by surveying recent forms of torture and how AI may figure in relation to them. The conclusion brings our indictment of the 'good AI' myth to the fore, as it looks at alternative ways to plan our common future.

In all of this, the reader will discern an urgency and a certain passion for a new episteme for humanity. It is the pain and suffering compounded by the delirious society that informs this tone and methodical empathy with the plight of those vulnerable strata of society that will be the first to suffer the full force of the age of Artificial Intelligence. The following chapters are a call to organise, in order to prevent that horrible future.

Notes

1. Some sections of this introduction are taken from a project that colleagues and I presented at the Venice Biennale of 2021. Thanks to the brilliant Future Studies Program and its director Jason Mohaghegh. See futurestudiesprogram.com accessed 12 June 2023. '1984 Original Trailer'. Available at www.youtube.com/watch?v=T8BA7adK6XA accessed 12 August 2023.
2. See also Michel Foucault, *Society Must Be Defended: Lectures at the Collège de France 1975–1976*, New York: Picador, 2003.
3. On modern disciplinary regimes, see also Michel Foucault, *Discipline and Punish: The birth of the prison*, London: Vintage, 1995.
4. Suzanne Smalley, 'A surveillance tower in Mexico becomes an unsettling landmark for privacy advocates', *The Record: Recorded Future News*, 16 October 2023. Available at https://therecord.media/torre-centinela-sentinel-tower-chihuahua-ciudad-juarez-texas-surveillance accessed 12 December 2023.
5. Ministerio de Seguridad, 'Resolución 710/2024, RESOL-2024-710-APN-MSG'. Available at www.boletinoficial.gob.ar/detalleAviso/primera/311381/20240729 accessed 2 August 2024.
6. Available at https://x.com/CELEUP/status/1818024600174789038 accessed 2 August 2024. See also Harriet Barber, 'Argentina will use AI to "predict future crimes" but experts worry for citizens' rights', *Guardian*, 1 August, 2024. Available at www.theguardian.com/world/article/2024/aug/01/argentina-ai-predicting-future-crimes-citizen-rights accessed 2 August 2024.
7. 'Bruce Lee: Be as water my friend'. Available at www.youtube.com/watch?v=cJMwBwFj5nQ accessed 12 January 2021.
8. Aldo Alvarez-Risco, Patricia Tapia, Shyla Del-Aguila-Arcentales, 'Sustainability and Urban Innovation by Smart City Implementation', in Bryan Christiansen and John D. Branch (eds.), *Analyzing International Business Operations in the Post-Pandemic Era*, London: Business Science Reference, 2022, pp. 227–253.

Introduction: The delirious society

9   For a rather more sensible recent case for smart cities, see David Ly, 'On the horizon for smart cities: How AI and IoT are transforming urban living', *Forbes*, 7 April 2023. Available at www.forbes.com/sites/forbestechcouncil/2023/04/07/on-the-horizon-for-smart-cities-how-ai-and-iot-are-transforming-urban-living/?sh=5053ffe77145 accessed 12 November 2023. For a counterargument to such data-driven projects, see Mirca Madianou, 'Nonhuman Humanitarianism: When "AI for good" can be harmful', *Information, Communication and Society*, Vol. 24, No. 6 (2021), pp. 850–868.

10 See also Shoshana Zuboff, *The Age of Surveillance Capitalism: The fight for a human future at the new frontier of power*, London: Profile Books, 2019.

11 Therefore traditional concepts in international relations have to be reconsidered. See also Arshin Adib-Moghaddam, 'World Politics after the War in Ukraine', *IPRI Journal*, Vol. XXII, No. 2 (2022), pp. 61–75. On the Iranian angle, see Arshin Adib-Moghaddam, *What is Iran? Domestic politics and international relations in five musical pieces*, Cambridge: Cambridge University Press, 2021.

12 See also Chris Westfall, 'As AI usage increases at work, searches for "AI girlfriend" up 2400%', *Forbes*, 4 October 2023. Available at www.forbes.com/sites/chriswestfall/2023/09/29/as-ai-usage-increases-at-work-searches-for-ai-girlfriend-up-2400/ accessed 11 October 2024.

13 *Ibid.* See also James Muldoon, 'Sex machina: In the wild west world of human-AI relationships, the lonely and vulnerable are most at risk', *The Conversation*, 9 October 2024. Available at https://theconversation.com/sex-machina-in-the-wild-west-world-of-human-ai-relationships-the-lonely-and-vulnerable-are-most-at-risk-239783?utm_medium=email&utm_campaign=Latest%20from%20The%20Conversation%20for%20October%209%202024%20-%203123331868&utm_content=Latest%20from%20The%20Conversation%20for%20October%209%202024%20-%203123331868+CID_4de502f707d435c532b30849704f9e29&utm_source=campaign_monitor_uk&utm_term=the%20highly%20unregulated%20world%20of%20human-AI%20relationships accessed 12 October 2024.

14 See Isabel Millar, *The Psychoanalysis of Artificial Intelligence*, London: Palgrave, 2021.

15 I have discussed this in chapter 5 of Arshin Adib-Moghaddam, *Is Artificial Intelligence Racist? The ethics of AI and the future of humanity*, London: Bloomsbury, 2023, pp. 97–114.

16 See among others Christian Enemark (ed.), *Ethics of Drone Strikes: Restraining remote-control killing*, Edinburgh: Edinburgh University Press, 2021.
17 For more on the dialectic between power and resistance, see Arshin Adib-Moghaddam, *On the Arab Revolts and the Iranian Revolution: Power and resistance today*, London: Bloomsbury, 2013. On the AI angle, see especially Rachel Adams, 'Can Artificial intelligence Be Decolonised?', *Interdisciplinary Science Reviews*, Vol. 46, No. 1–2 (2021), pp. 176–197.
18 See also Michael Kwet, 'Digital Colonialism: US Empire and the New Imperialism in the Global South', *Race and Class*, Vol. 60, No. 4 (2019), pp. 3–26.
19 The argument complements my previous book on the subject. See Adib-Moghaddam, *Is Artificial Intelligence Racist?*.
20 *Ibid.*
21 Charlene H. Chu, Simon Donato-Woodger, Shehroz S. Khan, Rune Nyrup, Kathleen Leslie, Alexandra Lyn, Tianyu Shi, Andria Bianchi, Samira Abbasgholizadeh Rahimi and Amanda Grenier, 'Age-Related Bias and Artificial Intelligence: A Scoping Review', *Humanities and Social Sciences Communications*, Vol. 10 (2023). Available at www.nature.com/articles/s41599-023-01999-y accessed 12 June 2024.
22 See also Safiya Umoja Noble, *Algorithms of Oppression: How search engines reinforce racism*, New York: New York University Press, 2018.
23 Jennifer Alsever, 'AI-powered speed hiring could get you an instant job, but are employers moving too fast?', *Fast Company*, 1 June 2023. Available at www.fastcompany.com/90831648/ai-powered-speed-hiring-could-get-you-an-instant-job-but-are-employers-moving-too-fast accessed 12 May 2024.
24 See Joseph B. Fuller, Manjari Raman, Eva Sage-Gavin and Kristen Hines, 'Hidden workers: Untapped talent', *Harvard Business School*, March 2023. Available at www.hbs.edu/managing-the-future-of-work/research/Pages/hidden-workers-untapped-talent.aspx accessed 12 May 2024.
25 See Sarah Roth and Becca Delbos, 'AI is causing massive hiring discrimination based on disability', *The Hill*, 8 April 2024. Available at https://thehill.com/opinion/technology/4576649-ai-is-causing-massive-hiring-discrimination-based-on-disability/ accessed 24 June 2024.

Introduction: The delirious society

26 Eileen O'Grady, 'Why AI fairness conversations must include disabled people', *Harvard Gazette*, 3 April 2024. Available at https://news.harvard.edu/gazette/story/2024/04/why-ai-fairness-conversations-must-include-disabled-people/ accessed 15 June 2024.

27 UNESCO, 'New UNESCO report warns that Generative AI threatens Holocaust memory', *UNESCO*, 18 June 2024. Available at www.unesco.org/en/articles/new-unesco-report-warns-generative-ai-threatens-holocaust-memory accessed 24 June 2024.

28 Vikram Dodd and Dan Milmo, 'AI could worsen epidemic of child sexual abuse, warns UK crime agency', *The Guardian*, 18 July 2023. Available at www.theguardian.com/society/2023/jul/18/ai-could-worsen-epidemic-of-child-sexual-abuse-warns-uk-agency accessed 16 November 2023.

29 *Ibid.*

30 See Adib-Moghaddam, Is Artificial Intelligence Racist?, 2023.

31 See for instance, Abeba Birhane, 'Algorithmic injustice: A relational ethics approach', *Patterns*, Vol. 2, No. 2 (2021). Available at www.sciencedirect.com/science/article/pii/S2666389921000155 accessed 25 January 2024.

32 See also 'Our Mission', Algorithmic Justice League, www.ajl.org/about accessed 22 February 2024.

33 Hamid Dabashi, *The Last Muslim Intellectual: The life and legacy of Jalal Al-e Ahmad*, Edinburgh: Edinburgh University Press, 2023, p. 172. See also Eskandar Sadeghi-Boroujerdi, 'Gharbzadegi, Colonial Capitalism and the Racial State in Iran', *Postcolonial Studies*, Vol. 24, No. 2, pp. 173–194.

34 Among many options, see Herbert Marcuse, *Towards a Critical Theory of Society*, London: Routledge, 2001 and Aníbal Quijano, *Aníbal Quijano: Foundational essays on the coloniality of power*, Durham: Duke University Press, 2024. For a relatively recent work on Al-e Ahmad, see Dabashi, *The Last Muslim Intellectual*.

1
Debugging machine ethics

We begin this chapter with a revelation.[1] I have started by arguing that the delirious society feeds off a mirage that is presented as reality. The reason we are in this predicament is straightforward: The data upon which everything we know is premised is tainted. In fact, we have been lied to by our teachers and some of our lecturers and professors, too. This may not have been deliberate. But there exists a regime of untruth, fuelled partially by ignorance and partially by wilful deception, which is aided and abetted by a set of foundational myths about our national history, politics, society and so on. We should not be surprised, thus, that our AI machines are biased.

The situation resembles the dynamics of a dysfunctional family, where everyone manipulates the others in order to win the argument. In such an environment, discussions are about winning and not about seeking the truth or educating oneself about the views of one's interlocutor. Our archives are dysfunctional exactly in this way, as they were stacked on ideological foundations and not on an inclusive dialogue with the world, especially during the European 'Enlightenment'. It was during this period when the history of the world was reduced to the demands of privileged White (and heterosexual) men, who literally rewrote the archives in their favour, expunging the presence of women and peoples of colour (the 'other') from the books. I am using 'White' as a non-'racial' category in my work, to denote a particularly hierarchical expression of the world that was codified in the science of racism in order to subjugate non-White populations. In this sense, more than anything else, being White as a concept in this study refers to a discourse feeding into a system of oppression and exploitation and does not refer to the colour of the skin as White Supremacists would argue in logical support of their racist agenda. As the *Black Skin, White Masks* analogy of Frantz Fanon famously highlighted in the 1940s with reference to the decolonial project in his native Martinique and later on informed by his anti-colonial activism in Algeria: Anyone can sustain and enable an oppressive, racist system when he accepts its exploitative premises In fact, as a 'Black' man, you may be a Trojan horse in this system, the native informant that no one sees coming.[2]

The crucial points for my line of argumentation is that the Enlightenment turned racism into a science and that our current AI universe must be seen as an extension of this techno-colonial system. The absence of a constructive dialogue with other sciences, world-views and philosophies in this period, and in many ways thereafter, explains quite clearly why societies in Europe and North America are particularly polluted by bad data so a whole set of residual racism, homo-transphobia and misogyny continues to rear its ugly head, especially during socio-economic crises. This is despite the recent movements towards better science, spearheaded by critical scholars with a sensitivity towards the way truths are invented as a mirage to fog our minds and to reinforce an essentially unjust and unequal social and political order.[3] In this age of AI, those residues of hate and bigotry are readily recrafted by neo-fascist movements all over the world. Therefore, their grip over our social media sites and their continued political success – in the name of the nation, the motherland, the religion, the party or any other dubious collectivisation that is turned into a psychotic formula for suppression – should not come as a surprise.

Ethical AI recoded

I have hypothesised that we are facing bad AI and discriminatory algorithms because of the way knowledge was inscribed into our archives during the European Enlightenment (and exported throughout the world through the violence of colonialism). The truths we were taught, in short, must be treated as a system of untruths. In order for this argument to hold, I must demonstrate how 'science' was invented, in particular with reference to social and political knowledge systems as I am essentially looking at the ethics of AI. This has implications for psychology, medicine, economics, pharmacy, anthropology, sociology, international relations, politics and all the other disciplines as well. But the root problem with bad AI can be traced back to the way knowledge was invented and taught to us in school and in many universities.

The idea of embedding ethical standards into a machine is already one of the main themes in the field of machine ethics.[4] However, 'debugging' our systems requires a philosophical approach that is in itself divested from the mistakes of the past. We cannot create ethical AI machines without an understanding of ethics that is globally informed, non-hierarchical and steeped in a philosophy of science that is non-hegemonic.

Debugging machine ethics

The ambition of this chapter is to initiate exactly that: A dialogue about a philosophical approach to machine ethics and/or AI studies more generally that is global right from the outset. To that end, I will chart how philosophy and the very meaning of 'ethics' were hijacked by European Enlightenment philosophers and how they can be repositioned in line with their global heritage. Ethical principles are never really confined to one locus. In particular, the idea that philosophy and its contribution to the meaning of ethics – or indeed any truth system – is not global in its constitution continues to be a widespread fallacy. In fact, it is an urgent matter to address this untruth, as it continues to be taught as 'scientific' at prestigious university departments even to the present day.[5]

Against this obstinate Eurocentrism, the present chapter demonstrates connections in a concrete and explicit manner, as it shows how some emancipatory themes in western philosophy, in particular in their Renaissance and Enlightenment manifestations, can be located in the ideas of philosophers in the 'east' and here in particular the *al-ḥhikma* tradition of the classical philosophers (e.g. Ibn Sina, Ibn Rushd [known in Latin as Averroes], Farabi), which developed in the Arab/Persian/Muslim realm and which in turn is imbued with Indian, Jewish, Hellenic, ancient Roman, North African and Zoroastrian traditions among other rhizomes of global thought. Naturally, there is no suggestion here that this is the only global angle from which to interrogate our tainted data. Some of this is limited by my own knowledge. But the present chapter does take advantage of recent strides in the social sciences and their emphasis on a critical and uncentred understanding of AI ethics.

Still marginal to the scholarly canon, some slow progress has been made to include non-western perspectives in machine ethics, for instance, experimenting with Dao, Confucian virtue perspectives or southern African *ubuntu* philosophy to explore novel meanings of universal community and humanity.[6] In this critical scholarship, there has emerged an emphasis on an integrative reading of world history in general and the production of systems of knowledge such as academic disciplines in particular.[7] My emphasis on philosophy and ethics as global thought serves as a contribution to that debate and to a better understanding of how exactly we can 'create a machine that follows an ideal ethical principle or set of principles in guiding its behaviour', as Susan Anderson, a pioneer of machine ethics, demanded.[8] In this way, the present chapter lays the groundwork for the rest of the book, as it identifies the power system that we are combating in order to carefully foster strategies of disruption, intervention and dissent. Our escape routes for the future can only be illuminated once we highlight the mistakes of the past that are overshadowing the blind spots of our present.

Centred philosophy versus universal ethics

Despite the institutionalised efforts to cleanse the western archives from any impingement of the 'other' during the European Enlightenment and in many ways thereafter, there have emerged in more recent decades intellectual movements that are reversing this 'theft of history'.[9] A wide range of critical theories and practices, from post-colonialism and post-structuralism to global history, global thought and comparative philosophies are reclaiming a seemingly lost intellectual tapestry that is spread across a global canvas.[10] Understood as a globalised system of thought, philosophy as the root discipline of the humanities/social sciences, as intellectual practice *and* everyday activism (and not so much as a structured discipline to be studied at university), lends itself to such a 'decolonial' debugging exercise perfectly, because philosophy gives us the ingredients that are necessary to code our AI machines responsibly. It is in this way that a global rooting of philosophy suggests an impulse that promises to break some of the Eurocentric shackles in machine ethics and AI studies more generally.[11]

If a philosopher's task is synonymous with the love for truth and aversion to falsehood, as the twelfth-century Hispanic-Muslim philosopher Ibn Rushd professed,[12] then philosophy chimes with our innate quest for betterment of the human condition, at least when philosophy is forcefully freed from the scourge of conformity and self-censorship which is prevalent even in contemporary academia.[13] Ibn Rushd followed a dotted line of philosophical thought from Oriental Greece to Occidental Persia and the Mediterranean. We are tracing such loose intellectual itineraries and relocating them at the same time, but not in order to create another hierarchy of knowledge or to recentre the debate about machine ethics around a particular period of time or an 'eastern' geography. Rather, we are trying to demonstrate that philosophy and its ethical underbelly carry a global heritage that has been denied by privileged gatekeepers, in many ways until today.

There is a second reason why philosophy qualifies as global thought that escapes geographical confinement in the west, or anywhere else for that matter. As an intellectual pursuit, philosophy (much in the same way as art) is located in historically contingent constellations that defy simple definitions. Of course, there have been efforts to define philosophy (and ethics). The etymology of 'philosophy' binds it historically to ancient Greece, itself a hybrid conglomerate of intercultural influences – *philein sophia*, or *philosophia*, meaning lover of wisdom. However, unless one continues to argue that it was only in ancient Athens or during the European Enlightenment that such love of wisdom was systematically expressed and taught, it is very difficult to hold on to the notion that western philosophy *is* philosophy and that it therefore has an exclusive hold on the meaning of ethics in the first place.

Even sympathetic approaches that market 'good AI' as the solution are problematic because they rest on ethical guidelines that are not inclusive, as the work of Tigard rightly flags.[14] If the global survey of Jobin *et al.* identifies transparency, justice, fairness, non-maleficence, responsibility and privacy as ethical principles that are globally cherished, in accordance with their quantitative study from 2019, then there is considerable controversy about the deeper meaning of these philosophical concepts and how they apply in different social and cultural contexts.[15]

Moreover, if philosophy is synonymous with the love of ethics, then there is evidence for such a pursuit in every civilisation that existed before Plato and Aristotle's contributions, for instance, in the *ganjis* of the Achaemenid empire (founded 550 BCE) in Persia – literally treasuries or spaces for books pertaining to Zoroastrian religion and scientific knowledge for medical and administrative purposes that in turn informed the houses of wisdom (*buyūt al-ḥikma*) immortalised in the 1001 nights depicting eighth-century Baghdad. Confucius and Sun Tzu, the sages of ancient China, philosophised about ethics over 100 years before Plato. Pre-Buddhist thinkers and Hindu ascetics presented comparably sophisticated philosophical systems of ethical thought that predated the ancient Greek philosophers.

More recent discoveries aid and abet this global heritage, for instance, in the 1990s when Peruvian researchers unearthed archaeological sites of the Norte Chico civilisation along the Peruvian coast whose truncated monuments, pyramids and complex governance systems suggest a dense philosophical heritage that dates back to the third millennium BCE, the earliest known in the western hemisphere. In fact, the trajectory of complex ideas such as philosophy, their travel itinerary so to speak, escapes any artificial confinement. Therefore, ethics does not have a singular origin and it shouldn't be taught as such. There is no text or object that could be consolidated as foundational despite stringent efforts in the 'western' canon to that end. Scholars of AI and machine ethics need to understand those 'bugs' in the system in order to equip themselves with the necessary 'software' to program responsible machines.

But even Eurocentric depictions which claim ethics (and related concepts such as art and architecture) for the west have failed to mute the critical promise that many philosophers believe in. The emergence of the aforementioned critical theories and their concomitant practices are contemporary manifestations of this rather more inclusive trend. Hence, the systematic effort to confine philosophy to the west and to gentrify the genealogy of ethics to remove any influence of the 'other' has failed, exactly because ethics has to escape the mould of any locus (or locality) in order to be accepted and legitimated. Therefore, whenever a limit is defined for philosophers and their deliberations on ethical machines, it must be immediately overturned as a conscious strategy to debug the data that feed into our AI systems. Otherwise, philosophy as the love for truth, the pursuit of wisdom (*ḥikma*), an exercise in freedom of thought, would yield a tyranny of misinformation or the folly of ideological tech-propaganda which has been exposed in various studies.[16]

Hybrid knowledge versus Eurocentrism

The gateways that will allow us to code ethical machines well educated in global thought can be adequately pushed open by focusing on the way classical 'Muslim' philosophers who lived in Europe, North Africa and throughout Asia dealt with contentious subjects such as rationality and knowledge. The limits of this chapter constrain me from giving a full account of these issues of course. But I hope to sketch a forward-looking modality in classical 'Muslim' philosophy which I think inherently critical and inclusive and therefore very useful to the debate about machine ethics.[17] In the philosophy of polymaths such as Abu Nasr Farabi (870–950 CE) and Ibn Sina ([known in Latin as Avicenna] 980–1037 CE), even in their poetry, life takes on a forward-looking modality adequate to this idea of the capacity for change which is always the prerequisite for any ethical theory based on reason. Their emphasis on learning and constant renewal is particularly useful to current debates about self-improving AI machines as they embed an optimistic call for the betterment of the human existence which was also at the heart of the European Enlightenment, in particular in its Kantian iteration encapsulated in his notion of *Vernunft* (reason). In that vein, in his *'uyūn al-ḥikma* Ibn Sina writes that *al-ḥikma* (which in his usage means the same as philosophy) is the 'perfection of the human soul through the conceptualisation [*taṣawwur*] of things and judgment [*taṣdīq*] of theoretical and practical realities to the measure of human ability'.[18] Learned individuals are encouraged to follow a path of finding this supreme knowledge, not least in order to transcend the humdrum affairs of their everyday reality and to attain a higher form of contentment and happiness.

Ibn Sina went on in his later writings to distinguish between Peripatetic philosophy and what he called 'Oriental philosophy' (*al-ḥikma al-mašriqiyya*) which was not based on ratiocination alone, but also engaged with revealed knowledge. This approach turned into an influential paradigm as it fed into the treatises of Sohravardi, and here especially his *Kitāb ḥikmat al-'išrāq*. The ultimate object here is the perfection of the intellectual faculties of the individual, who does not carry an exclusive identity – self-education as a strategy to connect with spirituality and the world surrounding us; philosophy as an exercise of self-expression. There is no realm of knowledge that is exclusive to 'Muslims' or any other religion/nation in the writings of Ibn Sina; no discernible schematic dichotomy that permeates his narratives. Ibn Sina searches for a supreme truth, not a supreme civilisation or race. He and many of his contemporaries managed to write their poetry and philosophy without the emergence of a discourse that would legitimise subjugation of the 'other', without a hysterical call for arms. In this sense their concept of reason and their ethical prescriptions were not identitarian. Undoubtedly, Ibn Sina would be an advocate of post-identity to battle ideological AI systems, as ideology always nurtures stringent boundaries between the elevated self and the lesser other. There is no such boundary in his ideas, no such political and social system built around the systematic oppression of another 'race'.

This emphasis on reason and rationality as a pursuit of ethical excellence that can be achieved by everyone who is sufficiently disciplined and qualified, can be discerned with equal force in the writings of Ibn Rushd (1126–1198). This Hispanic-Muslim genius took on the assertion of Plato that the Greeks

The myth of good AI

are superior to other peoples in their ability to receive wisdom by relocating wisdom to individuals in his own homeland of Andalusia and today's Egypt, Syria and Iraq. In Ibn Rushd too, then, we find hybridity. Like Ibn Sina before him, Ibn Rushd did not claim that only 'Muslims' can be philosophers or attain wisdom. Ibn Rushd explicitly affirmed the various loci of philosophical knowledge known to him. Such worldly consciousness may explain why systematic racism as a science taught at universities never really emerged in (western) Asia (and Africa and the Americas), and why it became a typically European abomination during modernity and the concomitant Enlightenment. It was in modern Europe, in other words, where the Platonic emphasis on the superiority of the Greeks was hijacked and turned into a racist mandate to rule over the 'barbarian other' thus invented.[19] Quite suddenly, Muslim (and Jewish) philosophy was cleansed from the archives as the standard philosophy books taught in the newly established, highly restrictive modern universities either did not acknowledge previous forms of philosophy or denigrated them as backward, even barbarian. Thus, standard histories of the discipline, such as Jean Félix Nourrisson's *Account of the Progress of Human Thought from Thales to Hegel* (1858) or Albert Stöckl's *Handbook of the History of Philosophy* (1870), didn't even mention Ibn Rushd, Ibn Sina, Maimonides or any other Muslim or Jewish philosophers.[20]

The trend continued well into the twentieth century.[21] Stunted by this ignorance of the global canons of knowledge, even Bertrand Russell, in his *History of Western Philosophy* (1946), was tempted to assume that 'Arabic philosophy is not important as original thought. Men like Avicenna and Averroes are essentially commentators.'[22] Apart from the fact that Russell conflates a supposedly 'ethnic' category such as 'Arab' with being

'Muslim', he relegates even Ibn Rushd (Averroes), who was born in southern Spain, out of the canon of western philosophy, indeed out of Europe itself, by deeming him Arab and therefore 'foreign'. Other contemporaries, such as Joseph Burgess, indulged in open mockery of these actively othered systems of knowledge. In his *Introduction to the History of Philosophy*, published in 1939, he claimed that the 'Western spirit ... is inclined to regard this Nirvana business as a lot of twaddle, unbecoming a man of common sense and sound judgment'.[23]

Such attitudes did not develop in systematic terms in the east or in the 'Global South'. It was only during the European Enlightenment and thereafter, when philosophy and other disciplines were claimed exclusively by heterosexual, White European men of a certain age and a privileged social class. The colonial period afforded them that luxury. Since then, this untruth of philosophy as a particularly western discipline has been mass-taught via a Eurocentric curriculum in the burgeoning modern educational system.[24] Consequently, there was no cadre of new philosophers emerging which could appreciate a hybrid understanding of knowledge-seeking, precisely because other philosophies were simply banished from the archives or categorised as 'unworthy' of study. No wonder then that today disciplines crucial to good or responsible AI, such as machine ethics, continue to grapple with an 'overarching ethical concern' about the way AI could negatively impact 'people's liberty, access to healthcare, housing, insurance, credit, employment, and transportation, among other social, economic, and political goods'.[25] This situation is particularly acute for minorities and it is rooted in our past.

So the problem rests on two ideological pillars: First a conception of ethics that is Eurocentric and not universal or global, and second a system of untruth that cordons off dialogues, symbiosis and consensus-seeking from sexual and ethnic minorities and other cultures more generally. As a result, ethical questions of the other have been literally 'whitewashed', certainly marginalised. Conversely, all of the classical philosophers from the east under scrutiny here were hybrid in their thinking, which is why they became polymaths, both poets and scientists, engaged in theology and mysticism, interested in philosophy and metaphysics as much as in the empirical world. Exactly because of their multicultural approach, they did not advance a concrete concept of 'identity' steeped in a racialised narrative that could signify a monologue within one race or that would organise their contemporaries within a militant, coherently formulated epistemology/ideology. Theirs was an emancipative philosophy almost entirely devoid of identity politics or a concrete and dichotomous notion of self and other. Hence their ideas qualify as 'global thought' imbued with a wide array of ethical viewpoints, and they should be read and studied as such in relation to today's controversy over AI ethics. In the case of these cosmopolitan Hispanics, Indians, Arabs and Persians, the historical circumstances they were writing in, the presence of functioning hybrid polities, and the absence of a concrete notion of racial identity did not merit, or require them to write in a stridently ideological mode or to establish a racist syntax for pseudo-ethical governance on that basis.[26] Theirs would be an AI discourse that is essentially pre-ideological.

We have established that in terms of method, too, the classical philosophers were not mono-ethical. They employed complex methods drawn from various knowledge systems: Zoroastrian, African, nomadic, Persian, Arab, Indian, Central Asian, Jewish, Christian, Hellenic, Roman etc. Their epistemological diversity allowed them to examine how truth conditions can be rationalised through the study of language, judgement, nature, syllogisms, deductions and inductions. *Falsafa* (philosophy) was considered to lead to the knowledge of all existing things qua existent (*'ašyā' al-mawǧūda bi-mā hiya mawǧūda*) and philosophy itself was deemed to be the art of arts and the science (*'ilm*) of sciences. What came surreptitiously into existence in the writings of these philosophers, in short, was nothing less than the renewal of philosophy as a critical practice, world-view, ethics *and* form of everyday conduct. For Ibn Rushd, as indicated, these qualities of 'wisdom' should not be thought the prerogative and purview of one class of humans.

> This opinion would only be correct if there were but one class of humans disposed to the human perfections and especially to the theoretical ones. It seems that this is the opinion that Plato holds of the Greeks. However, even if we accept that they are the most disposed by nature to receive wisdom, we cannot disregard [the fact] that individuals like these—i.e. those disposed to wisdom—are frequently to be found. You find this in the land of the Greeks and its vicinity, such as this land of ours, namely Andalus, and Syria and Iraq and Egypt, albeit this existed more frequently in the land of the Greeks.[27]

Before Ibn Rushd set out this rather more inclusive 'history of wisdom' (and by extension philosophy and ethics), Farabi traversed and falsified similar Platonic boundaries in a related debate about 'origins'. From the perspective of this 'Persianate-Muslim' thinker, the lineage of philosophy can be traced from the Chaldeans to Iraq and to Egypt and thereafter to the Greeks from whom the Syrians and finally the Arabs retrieved it.[28] In addition, Maimonides, the Hispanic-Jewish contemporary of

The myth of good AI

Ibn Rushd, deemed the Persians, Syrians and Greeks 'the most learned and expert of the nations'.[29] Maimonides, too, was expunged from the western literature due to his Jewish heritage.

It has been established in the scholarly literature on the subject that all of this happened in close association with the Aristotelian and Platonic tradition and ancient philosophy described as Greek in general. But even today, certainly in the standard disciplinary engagement with philosophy, there is no systematic effort to theorise philosophy as global thought, as an amalgamation of the innate quests of a select number of humans dotted throughout world history to seek reasoned knowledge and an ethical system that serves humanity. In too many schools and universities all over the world, pupils and students (including in machine ethics) are still educated to believe either a nationalised narrative or an ethnocentric one. Both tend to express a hegemony of knowledge that is both untrue and laden with various forms of misogyny, homophobia and racism, exactly because such forms of political and social discourses are by definition exclusionary.[30]

Dei ex machina

We have to dig deeper to unearth the cyphers that could inform a better understanding of philosophy in our contemporary debates about AI ethics. Without minority representation, as a recent *MIT Technology Review* article rightly points out, the various declarations, calls for AI ethics boards and internal audits will continue to 'produce a global vision for AI ethics that reflects the perspectives of people in only a few regions of the world … there's a clear lack of regional diversity in many AI advisory boards, expert panels, and councils appointed by

Debugging machine ethics

leading international organizations'.[31] Things are bad, even in places where one expects inclusivity, as I have experienced in my own research and exposure to some UN agencies focusing on AI. For instance, at the time of writing the expert group advising the AI for Children project administered by UNICEF has no representative from the so-called 'Middle East', Africa and Asia – areas of the world that actually have the highest concentration of young adults and children.

We have argued that our scientific institutions tasked with teaching the truth continue to be hampered by a set of exclusionary Eurocentric myths. Take the aforementioned Burgess: In his influential introduction to philosophy, he articulated a general cliché about the classical philosophers of the east that is still regurgitated today. Burgess was certainly also under the influence of the German giant of idealist thought George Wilhelm Friedrich Hegel (1770–1831) who relegated 'Muslims' to an infantile stage of history because of their supposed 'God complex', as we will discuss further in the next chapter. In a similar vein, Burgess wrote that, 'Occidental thought ... is impatient with philosophies that hint of other-worldliness because it wishes to keep its feet firmly planted on solid, scientifically supported ground.'[32] Therefore, according to Burgess, Europeans could afford to ignore the east. In this way, western thought was rendered scientific, whereas the rest of the world was declared 'superstitious'.

Patience is required for an empathetic ethical system to come to the fore and certainly for good scholarship to be archived for future generations dealing with AI. It is true that for the classical philosophers of the so-called 'Muslim Enlightenment', in many ways up until Ibn Khaldun (1332–1406), reality is not exhausted by explaining what offers itself to immediate knowledge and perception. An understanding of the world around us must also include an aspect of future potentiality, a 'utopia' wherein the discrepancy between the present and the future opens up. This is why, in the philosophy of Farabi and especially in Ibn Sina's intricate *Daneshnameh-ye Alai (Treatise on Knowledge)*, philosophy takes on a forward-looking modality adequate to this idea of the capacity for 'extraterrestrial' change as indicated. In Ibn Sina's view, the contingent existent (*mumkin al-wuğūd*) is always relative to the necessary being (*wāğib al-wuğūd*).[33] Within such a dialectic, one is alerted to know the present in order to bridge the gap between the ontology surrounding us and the transcendental promise which is relegated to an extraterrestrial deity, without, however, forcing a total causality upon this process. If Burgess had cared to dig deeper into the true history of philosophy, he would have been forced to acknowledge that the world Ibn Sina conceptualised is essentially secular, exactly because that God is placed in another realm of existence, not out of political expediency, but out of acknowledgement that total knowledge can never be attained, thus creating the impulse for continuous betterment of the human condition in the here and now.

Furthermore, in all that happened eight centuries before Nietzsche proclaimed the 'death of God', we fail to see a fundamental, ontological, hermeneutical or epistemological boundary to the ideas of the most prominent Enlightenment thinkers. The idea of Descartes that reason is the chief source of human knowledge and that God is displaced by what can be experienced through the senses is comparable to Ibn Sina's view that humankind is in charge of its destiny, as God occupies another realm which is by definition unattainable. As we are witnessing forms of AI worship and religious organisation curated around the prospect of a superior Artificial General Intelligence (AGI)

Debugging machine ethics

that is immediately present in our everyday life, we need this wider pool of understanding about the 'location' of God. If God can be an AI machine, as some people already believe, shouldn't we at least consider the dangers of some sort of AI fundamentalism that could be far more destructive than any religious extremism that we have encountered so far?[34] I would say yes, quite because an AI God would be all-encompassing – that God would be entirely capable of governing our everyday life and visibly so given its presence in the here and now, facilitated by the devices we use on a daily basis.

Here, John Locke's (1632–1704) view that the chief source of knowledge is the ability to observe and experience our surroundings, and that religious dogma is therefore superfluous, is another important signpost in the debate about the location of the traditional, non-AI God. For Locke, God is not here – for AI worshippers, he would be. For Farabi, as articulated in his *Enumeration of the Sciences*, which relegates religious knowledge to theology (*fiqh*) and jurisprudence (*kalām*), philosophy is the master discipline overlaying every other knowledge system, even Islamic law itself.[35] For many AI enthusiasts, philosophy is nothing but a nuisance. Instead they worship a *deus ex machina*,

> which according to some in the transhumanist movement, advocates for the enhancement of the human condition in terms of both its longevity and cognition. This AI-centric God will be made in the *image* and *likeness* of humans *by* humans simulating the famous *imago Dei* of Genesis 1:2.[36]

Machine gods already exist, then. These *dei ex machina* have profound implications for ethics as we know it and the moral foundations of being human at all. When the boundary of our cognitive faculties is breached by the Neuralink brain-computer

The myth of good AI

interface that Elon Musk sponsors, we essentially merge with AI machines, exposing ourselves to AI Gods that would have direct access to our thinking in the frontal lobe of our brain, not in some abstract realm that traditional religions would deem to be the soul. This human-machine interface aiming to achieve Singularity, the creation that will supersede us and which is celebrated by so-called futurists such as Raymond Kurzweil, is a direct threat to our free will, which undergirds our democracies and their core ambitions such as human rights and human dignity.[37] In such a posthumanist AI world, ideal governance would not be provided by what Ibn Rushd – in clear reference to Plato – would consider a philosopher: A 'king, lawgiver' who could also be considered an Imam because 'Imam in Arabic means one who is followed in his actions. He who is followed in these actions by which he is a philosopher, is an Imam in the absolute sense.'[38] In the posthumanist AI world, the happy-city conceptualised by Ibn Rushd as the democratic archetype would die a slow but certain death. Ibn Rushd states that the democracy of this happy-city 'is the one of which most of the multitude hold that it is the city to be admired, for every man asserts on the basis of unexamined opinion that he deserves to be free'.[39] Those humans who contemplate a Neuralink implant for no real medical reason don't seem to think that they deserve to be free – therefore they become a potential danger to everyone else.

Apart from a direct threat to our ambition to be free, *dei ex machina*, as indicated, transpose God back into our life, even into our physiognomy via human-machine interface projects such as Musk's dangerous Neuralink. One of the achievements of the European Enlightenment was that it furthered previous intellectual advances which displaced religion from dictating everyday life. In terms of method, denying our ability to sense God was crucial to that end. When robots can implant a microchip in our brain that would connect us directly to a *deus ex machina*, the eighteenth-century revelation of Immanuel Kant that even theological knowledge is not possible – because it is only our surrounding reality in terms of time, space, causation and substance that can be conceptualised and therefore systematically ordered – seems a crucial reminder about the unavailability of God. Such ideas fundamentally constitute the secular mindset. Everything that goes beyond this reality, Kant argues, i.e. the otherworldly, can't be grasped, whether through theology or metaphysics (or a human-machine interface for that matter).

Furthermore, even before his *Critique of Pure Reason* and its more secular musings, Kant framed the concept of God in terms of the *allgenugsam*, the single all-sufficient being. This is very comparable to the *wāǧib al-wuǧūd* idea of Ibn Sina, the first cause upon which the physical world rests. Kant's idea that the perfection of the physical universe surrounding us is 'an undeniable proof of their (i.e., all physical things) common first origin, which must be an all-sufficient highest mind in which the natures of things were designed in accordance with unified purposes'[40] is a clear nod to the first cause that Ibn Sina's theory rested upon about seven centuries before Kant. Such an engagement with an unattainable, otherworldly deity binds east and west together in a tango with an unavailable God. This deletion of divine intervention could be a starting point to combat future AI fundamentalists and their professed ability to 'sense' God via their robotic interfaces. You can't sense God. What you are feeling is a phantasmal mirage, carefully programmed in order to turn you into a customer.

The world of the philosopher and poet Omar Khayyam (1048–1123), one of the most prominent students of Ibn Sina, is a good place to unravel further the contribution of the idea of God to secular philosophy and to offer the reader a more global understanding of (machine) ethics. The world-view of Khayyam can be called critical and secular because of the libertarian momentum that his concept of God elicits. To his mind, God was the necessary being, or *mumtani' al-wuğūd* in Arabic (Ibn Sina termed God *wāğib al-wuğūd* as indicated). By necessity, human beings were relative to this otherworldly constant – this *allgenugsam* – in exactly the same way as Kant conceptualised it centuries later. Other concepts such as freedom – hijacked from global thought and claimed to be western only – are equally central to the ideas of Khayyam. In the world portrayed in his poetry, living a free life is immanent to existence because, in relation to God, reality is regarded as socially engineered. In the absence of a perfect order ordained by God, individuals are at liberty to live their lives in pursuit of freedom and happiness. For Khayyam the absence of the necessary being, or the *allgenugsam* in Kantian terms, continuously entices the relative being, that is the individual, throughout his/her pursuit of ethical betterment. This is the exact opposite of the perfectionism that is propounded by the priests of the futurist AI movement, which is based on desires 'to get more neocortex … to be funnier … better at music [and] sexier', as Raymond Kurzweil promises with a good dose of techno-hysteria.[41]

Conversely, in Khayyam's world there is freedom exactly because, in relation to the otherworldly realm, which remains unattainable, this world we are living in is intransigently complex and not comprehensible in its entirety, prompting us to seek more knowledge in pursuit of happiness, not with a short-cut human-machine interface implanted in our brains, but through real education and contemplative thought. Here, Khayyam reveals himself as an early postmodernist. He was convinced that the world surrounding us is constructed, because the realm of actual reality belongs to an unattainable deity. In other words, in his philosophy Khayyam alerted us to the fact that, relative to the *allgenugsam*, the socially engineered world surrounding the individual can be curated to further our happiness, precisely because the ultimate truth escapes us anyway.

All of this may explain why Khayyam lived the life of a philosopher rebel, uplifted by wine and his love for poetry. Khayyam expressed his alien reality, thus giving the lie to any notion of religion (including Islam) as a total system immune from the grim impact of historical events. As the inspirational Mutazillite movement centred around Basra and Baghdad professed between the eighth and tenth centuries, even the 'Koran, as the speech of God, was created'.[42] Hence, religion was thought to be historically contingent; and organised religion was considered hypocritical and ultimately senseless. In the words of Khayyam:

> The sphere upon which mortals come and go,
> Has no end nor beginning that we know;
> And none there is to tell us in plain truth:
> Whence do we come and whither do we go.[43]

The failure of Khayyam to redeem himself, the fact that neither his poetry nor his drunkenness could bring him closer to God, is also, paradoxically, the source of the irresistible ethical merit of his poetry and philosophy. Khayyam presaged the idea that the individual is constantly obliged to bridge the gap between this alien world and the necessary realm designated as God's, only to be disappointed that none of the religious obligations work to that end:

> What matters if I feast, or have to fast?
> What if my days in joy or grief are cast?
> Fill me with Thee, O Guide! I cannot ken
> If breath I draw returns or fails at last.[44]

There would be no room in the ethics of Khayyam for an attainable AGI deity that can be sensed through an artificial neural pathway implanted in our bodies. God is by definition unattainable – oneness with God is the 'impossible ontology' or *mumtani' al-wuğūd* in Ibn Sina's words. In this way, Khayyam and the Avicennian tradition tried to establish an essentially free world-view, which also explains the non-religious, rather hedonistic lifestyle that these free-thinkers lived. God as *mumtani' al-wuğūd* – the impossible ontology which explains the inherently secular order – chimes well with Kant's notion that an 'ethical community' requires God as the 'presupposition of another idea, namely, of a higher moral being through whose universal organization the forces of single individuals, insufficient on their own, are united for a common effect'.[45] For Kant as well, the idea of God as an unattainable ontology requires that we determine our own fate – no religious doctrine or AGI machine can help us to establish a divine order on earth.

This idea of Kant's, then, connects to Khayyam's assertion that humanity is dependent on the idea of God as a divine, unattainable moral entity.[46] Mysticism (Sufism), poetry, the arts and above all philosophy become the inevitable routes to seek respite from the results of oppressive systems and to create an ethical social and political order in the happy-city. These pursuits held out the promise of a realm of consciousness where the individual could at last find an image of equilibrium, of sensuous pleasure that would rescue her from the antinomies of her present existence. As such, philosophy (and poetry) embody a much-perfected form of ontological negation. In this way, for Khayyam and Kant, the idea of God functions as a propeller for a productive form of criticism and as an incubator for secular expressions of critique and philosophy. This relegation of God to a metaphysical no man's land would also explain why some of these classical philosophers were harassed, and in the case of the Iraqi-Persian mystic Mansur al-Hallaj (858–922) executed, for their 'heresy' in relation to the orthodoxy of the day. Khayyam was acutely aware of this danger:

> The secrets which my book of love has bred,
> Cannot be told for fear of loss of head;
> Since none is fit to learn, or cares to know,
> 'Tis better all my thoughts remain unsaid.[47]

In our fight for machine ethics and responsible AI systems that do not become avatars for new forms of techno-fundamentalism, incorporating philosophy into a global movement is necessary. For too long the global similarities set out in this chapter, which would prompt every thorough teacher to check a paper for plagiarism, never really entered any of the standard texts about the history of philosophy. All of this makes one sympathise with those intellectuals who have argued that the theft of knowledge during the European Enlightenment was a convenient political strategy to legitimise the civilising mission at the heart of colonial conquests and its various underlying racisms. Certainly, by today's standards, the godfather of the

The myth of good AI

Vernunftsgedanke, Immanuel Kant, *was* a racist. Undoubtedly, contemporary critical scholars correctly argue that the philosophy of luminaries such as John Locke (1632–1704), David Hume (1711–1776) *et al.*, foundational as they were for the European Enlightenment, must be indicted because they believed and tried to explain 'scientifically' that Black, Indigenous and other peoples were not only barbarians, but racially inferior and therefore in need of correction by European civilisation. This is the source of the massive amount of bad data, taught to us as science, that continues to pollute our algorithms today. It is the fertile ground in which strategies of psycho-codification, microbial surveillance and posthuman warfare take root.

All of this has been explored in recent critical scholarship about the Enlightenment and provides some useful foundations for a new understanding of ethics in this emergent age of Artificial Intelligence.[48] We need to codify these valuable ingredients into viable algorithms and software empathetic enough to debug machine ethics from the ethnocentric datasets nestled in our archives. This chapter has served as an example for the type of thinking needed on the 'good AI' oversight boards that Google, Meta, Apple, Microsoft etc. advertise with such great fanfare. In their meetings, the manuals for ethics need to be rewritten. There needs to be a worldly scholar alerting the programmers to the Kyoto School and its frontal interrogation of (western) modernity; its definitions of ethics commencing with Nishida Kitaro and his invitation for mutual critique and acknowledgement between different world-views steeped in ancient Mahayana Buddhist ideas.[49] This scholar would point to the incredibly beautiful merit in the non-foundational notions of Nagarjuna Buddhism and its emphasis on emptiness (*sunyata*),[50] which negates any belief in fixed identities and their hierarchical abuse in the name of the nation or race.[51] If we want to talk about ethical AI, we had better start with good science.

The idea of *Pachamama* or mother earth in Andean philosophy promises comparably dialogical merit, as it denotes an inherent and insoluble bond between humanity, nature and the wider cosmos. Such an approach is very meaningful for the present environmental insurgency against global warming. The ethics boards of the tech-giants may not like to hear it, but the environmental impact of the massively carbon-dependent AI industry is not being adequately addressed by the 'good AI' lobby. A recent study from researchers at the AI start-up Hugging Face established that generating one AI-powered image takes the same amount of energy as fully charging your mobile phone.[52] These huge energy demands of AI explain why Amazon and Google are buying into nuclear power plants to fuel their extremely energy-intensive data centres. This nexus between AI and nuclear technology is another dangerous arena that is largely being ignored. This ongoing alienation from the environment/nature is a clear consequence of the European Enlightenment and its legacies, which are largely devoid of a holistic view of life that would appreciate the spirit of concepts such as *Pachamama* and their incredible merit for our attitudes towards nature and the cosmos. The challenge for everyone is clear, then: We need to craft our everyday life, our subjectivity, in close cross-fertilisation with global ideas. Only with this conjoined spirit can we fundamentally shape this age of AI with truly human empathy and an ethical system that speaks to our universally shared sentiments.

Notes

1. Sections of this chapter are adapted from Arshin Adib-Moghaddam, 'Eastern Origins of Western Philosophy: Against Eurocentricism', *Folia Orientalia*, Vol. 60 (2023), pp. 311–327.
2. See also Frantz Fanon, *Black Skin, White Masks*, London: Penguin, 2019 and Hamid Dabashi, *Brown Skin, White Masks*, London: Pluto, 2011. On the possibility of resistance, see Arshin Adib-Moghaddam, 'Can the (Sub)altern Resist?: A Dialogue between Foucault and Said', in Ian Netton (ed.), *Orientalism Revisited: Art, land, voyage*. Abingdon: Routledge, 2013, pp. 33–54.
3. With reference to AI, see most recently: Dan McQuillan, *Resisting AI: An anti-fascist approach to Artificial Intelligence*, Bristol: Bristol University Press, 2022.
4. See among others Patrick Lin, Keith Abney and George A. Bekey (eds.), *Robot Ethics: The ethical and social implications of robotics. Intelligent robotics and autonomous agents*, London: MIT Press, 2014; Michael Anderson and Susan Leigh Anderson (eds.), *Machine Ethics*, Cambridge: Cambridge University Press, 2011; Wendel Wallach, Stan Franklin, Colin Allen, 'A Conceptual and Computational Model of Moral Decision Making in Human and Artificial Agents', *Topics in Cognitive Science*, Vol. 2, No. 3 (2010), pp. 454–485.
5. See Bret W. Davis, 'Dislodging Eurocentrism and Racism from Philosophy', *Comparative and Continental Philosophy*, Vol. 9, No. 2 (2017), pp. 115–118.
6. Pak Hang-Wong, 'Dao, Harmony, and Personhood: Towards a Confucian ethics of technology', *Philosophy & Technology*, Vol. 25, No. 1 (2011), pp. 67–86; Christopher S. Wareham, 'Artificial Intelligence and African Conceptions of Personhood', *Ethics and Information Technology*, Vol. 23, No. 2 (2021), pp. 127–136.
7. See among others John Hobson, *The Eastern Origins of Western Civilisation*, Cambridge: Cambridge University Press, 2004.
8. Anderson and Anderson (eds.), *Machine Ethics*, p. 22.
9. The phrase is from Jack Goody, *The Theft of History*, Cambridge: Cambridge University Press, 2007.
10. See the contributions in Jason Mohaghegh and Lucian Stone (eds.), *Manifestos for World Thought*, London: Rowman & Littlefield, 2017.
11. On the emancipatory promise of art and philosophy, see Theodor W. Adorno, *Aesthetic Theory*, London: Bloomsbury, 2013.

Debugging machine ethics

12 Averroes, *Averroes on Plato's Republic*, trans. Ralph Lerner, London: Cornell University Press, 1974, p. 72.
13 On the qualities of a philosopher, see *ibid.*, pp. 72–73.
14 See Daniel W. Tigard, 'There is No Techno-Responsibility Gap' *Philosophy & Technology*, Vol. 34, No. 1 (2020), pp. 589–607 and Daniel W. Tigard, 'Responsible AI and Moral Responsibility: A common appreciation', *AI and Ethics*, Vol. 1, No. 2 (2020), pp. 113–117.
15 See Anna Jobin, Marcello Ienca, Effy Vayena, 'The Global Landscape of AI Ethics Guidelines', *Nature Machine Intelligence*, Vol. 1, No. 2 (2019), pp. 389–399.
16 See among many others the classic Paul Virilio, *The Administration of Fear*, London: Semiotext(e), 2012.
17 I am using quotation marks around 'Muslim' because the classical philosophers under scrutiny here did not live an orthodox religious life, nor did their ideas have particularly Islamic connotations. Nonetheless, they self-identified as 'Muslim'.
18 Ibn Sina, *Fontes Sapientiae (uyun al-hikmah)*, Abdurrahman Badawied (ed.), Cairo: no publisher, 1954, p. 16.
19 See also Arshin Adib-Moghaddam, 'A (Short) History of the Clash of Civilizations', *Cambridge Review of International Affairs*, Vol. 21, No. 2 (2008), pp. 217–234.
20 On similar omissions, see also Lloyd Strickland, 'How Western Philosophy Became Racist', Institute of Art and Ideas, 10 January 2019. Available at https://iai.tv/articles/the-racism-of-the-western-philosophy-canon-auid-1200 accessed 12 January 2023.
21 See also Samar Attar, 'Suppressed or Falsified History? The Untold Story of Arab-Islamic Rationalist Philosophy', in N. R. F, Al-Rodhan (ed.), *The Role of the Arab-Islamic World in the Rise of the* West, London: Palgrave Macmillan, 2012, pp. 116–143.
22 Bertrand Russell, *History of Western Philosophy*, Collectors Edition, London: Taylor and Francis, 2013, p. 346.
23 Joseph Burgess, *Introduction to the History of Philosophy*, London: McGraw-Hill Book Company, 1939, p. 17.
24 See also Bret W. Davis, 'Dislodging Eurocentrism and Racism from Philosophy', *Comparative and Continental Philosophy*, Vol. 9, No. 2 (2017), pp. 115–118.
25 Robert Shanklin, Michael Samorani, Shannon Harris and Michael A. Santoro, 'Ethical Redress of Racial Inequities in AI: Lessons from decoupling machine learning from optimization in medical

appointment scheduling', *Philosophy and Technology*, Vol. 35, No. 4 (2022), pp. 1–19.

26 Of course, the violence exercised over the Muslim world during the colonial period changed all that and it was then that 'Islamism' was born. For more, see Adib-Moghaddam, 'A (Short) History of the Clash of Civilizations'.

27 Averroes, *Averroes on Plato's Republic*, p. 13.

28 *Ibid.*, p. 13.

29 *Ibid.*, p. 13.

30 See Susan E. Babbitt and Sue Campbell (eds.), *Racism and Philosophy*, London: Cornell University Press, 1999.

31 Abhishek Gupta and Victoria Heath, 'AI ethics groups are repeating one of society's classic mistakes', *MIT Technology Review*, 14 September 2020. Available at www.technologyreview.com/2020/09/14/1008 323/ai-ethics-representation-artificial-intelligence-opinion/ accessed 12 February 2022.

32 Burgess, *Introduction to the History of Philosophy*, p. 17

33 See Seyyed Hossein Nasr with Mehdi Aminrazavi (eds.), *An Anthology of Philosophy in Persia. Vol. I: From Zoroaster to 'Umar Khayyām*. Oxford: Oxford University Press: 1999, pp. 196ff.

34 See also Neil McArthur, 'Gods in the machine? The rise of artificial intelligence may result in new religions', *The Conversation*, 15 March 2023. Available at https://theconversation.com/gods-in-the-machine-the-rise-of-artificial-intelligence-may-result-in-new-religions-201068 accessed 24 November 2023.

35 See Muhsin S. Mahdi, *Alfarabi and the Foundation of Islamic Philosophy*, London: University of Chicago Press, 2001.

36 M.G. Michael, Katina Michael and Terri Bookman, 'Can God be an AI with robo-priests?', *Technology and Society*, 15 April 2023. Available at https://technologyandsociety.org/can-god-be-an-ai-with-robo-priests/ accessed 22 November 2023 (emphasis in the original).

37 *Ibid.*

38 Averroes, *Averroes on Plato's Republic*, p. 2.

39 *Ibid.*, p. 111.

40 Quoted in 'Kant's Philosophy of Religion', *Stanford Encyclopedia of Philosophy*, 22 June 2004. Available at https://plato.stanford.edu/entries/kant-religion/#:~:text=With%20the%20introduction%20of%20Transcendental,"needs"%20of%20practical%20reason.

41 Quoted in Patrick Caughill, 'Elon Musk eviscerates people who discuss "A.I. Gods"', *Futurism*, 24 October 2017. Available at https://futurism.com/elon-musk-eviscerates-people-who-discuss-a-i-gods accessed 10 January 2023.

42 Majid Fakhry, *A History of Islamic Philosophy*, 3rd edition, New York: Columbia University Press, 2014, p. 63.

43 Omay Khayyam, *The Quatrains of Omar Khayyam*, Edward H. Whinfield (trans., ed.), London: Routledge, 2001, p. 132. See also Mehdi Aminrazavi, 'Martin Heidegger and Omar Khayyam on the Question of "Thereness" (*Dasein*), in Anna-Teresa Tymieniecka (ed.), *Islamic Philosophy and Occidental Phenomenology on the Perennial Issue of Microcosm and Macrocosm*, Dordrecht: Springer, 2006, pp. 283ff.

44 Khayyam, *The Quatrains of Omar Khayyam*, p. 144.

45 Immanuel Kant, *Religion within the Bounds of Bare Reason* (trans. G. di Giovanni as *Religion within the Boundaries of Mere Reason* in *Religion and Rational Theology*, ed. A. W. Wood and G. di Giovanni), Cambridge: Cambridge University Press, 1996, p. 97. See also Stephen R. Palmquist, 'Kant's Religious Argument for the Existence of God: The ultimate dependence of human destiny on divine assistance', *Faith and Philosophy*, Vol. 26, No. 1 (2009), pp. 3–22 (p. 10).

46 Seyyed Hossein Nasr, *The Islamic Intellectual Tradition in Persia*, Mehdi Aminrazavi (ed.), London: Curzon, 1996, p. 81.

47 Omar Khayyam, *The Nectar of Grace: Omar Khayyām's life and works*, S. G. Tirtha (ed.), Allahabad: Government Central Press, 1941, p. 266.

48 Edward Said's work continues to gain currency with reference to critiques of the Enlightenment. See, for instance, Said, *Culture and Imperialism*, 1994. See also Dabashi's work, such as Hamid Dabashi, *Europe and Its Shadows: Coloniality after empire*, London: Pluto Press, 2019.

49 See, among others, Hisao Matsumaru, Yoko Arisaka and Lucy Christine Schultz (eds.), *Tetsugaku Companion to Nishida Kitarō*, New York: Springer, 2022.

50 See, among others, Graham Priest, 'The Structure of Emptiness', *Philosophy East and West*, Vol. 59, No. 4 (2009), pp. 467–480 and Graham Priest, *One*, Oxford: Oxford University Press, 2014.

51 I am thankful to one of the reviewers for drawing my attention to some of these themes.

52 See Melissa Heikillä, 'AI's carbon footprint is bigger than you think: Generating one image takes as much energy as fully charging your smartphone', *MIT Technology Review*, 5 December 2023. Available at www.technologyreview.com/2023/12/05/1084417/ais-carbon-footprint-is-bigger-than-you-think/ accessed 11 June 2024.

2
Eugenic racism

We have argued that there was a conscious and concerted effort to claim knowledge systems such as philosophy for Europe, as a means to buttress a hegemonic discourse. In its political manifestation, this Eurocentrism fed into the colonialist *zeitgeist* and its underlying misogyny and racism. It was simultaneously argued that some of this history underlies our current AI data problems. Even those readers who deny that there is a link between the untruth professed by Eurocentrism must acknowledge that the examples curated for this study provide enough evidence to support the assumption that by denying the global loci of world thought, Enlightenment philosophers were implicated in an ignorant denial of global history. These legacies continue to cast a dark shadow on our current age of Artificial Intelligence, explaining the recurrence of algorithmic bias, which some scholars have rightly called a form of techno-oppression.[1]

All of these instances of wilful distortion feed our suspicion that the Enlightenment project was also a grand ideological misnomer and a fatalistic betrayal of science that contributed to several tragedies in European and human history that persist in many ways to this day. Perhaps this trend did indeed start with

The myth of good AI

Immanuel Kant, as the important work of Lloyd Strickland, Jia Wang and others suggests.[2] But for our argument, it is central to underline that all knowledge systems, and certainly the so-called 'western' sciences, are rooted in global loci of thought. Hence, our common archives have to be reconsidered and rewritten as global thought if we are truly concerned with how we can code our machines with good, inclusive data. This will involve a process of re-education based on new knowledge systems drawn from the 'other' archives beyond our libraries.

The ambition of this chapter is to continue to advocate global thought as a philosophical approach to critical AI studies. At this new dawn, we must avoid the mistakes of the past. If we are to study AI from a truly critical perspective and to hold some of the big tech companies to account, then we need an intellectual movement that is inclusive, not only in political terms, but based on a science that is steeped in new rhizomes of thought that are cleansed of racism and the untruths nestled in our archives and increasingly in the AI algorithms governing our lives. In order to continue to find the right solutions, let us continue to link the mistakes of the past to the predicaments of the present in order to identify opportunities for the future.

Geopolitics old and new

The Enlightenment afforded the newly invented west a unique opportunity: To spread the ideas of predominantly 'White' (heterosexual) men across the entire world. Spatial elements are always present in the west's self-definition, today reflected in standard terms such as 'universal human rights', 'the international community', 'the norms-based international order' and 'civilised nations'. The emerging norms governing AI are being developed in that contentious space, too. In this way, geopolitical space has repeatedly served as a directed movement of destiny over foreign territories defined by the dominant imperial classes. That is how the national and imperialist *Grossraum* was born,[3] which has transmuted into a form of 'eugenicist geopolitics' that is increasingly governing not only physical territory, but our bodies and cognition. It is this transmission belt from the old geopolitics – which was concerned with territory – to this new eugenicist geopolitics – which psycho-codifies our minds – that is central to this chapter.

We have established that the spatial organisation of the world in favour of a privileged caste of men has been a central outcome of the European Enlightenment. The colonisation of North America extended that privilege into an invented space that we call the west even today. This Eurocentric spatial organisation of the world was necessary for the White European immigrants to North America, Australia and elsewhere who rationalised their colonial project with ideas of expansion and 'transcendental sovereignty', the universal mission ordained by God to promote justice. The famed French philosophers Gilles Deleuze and Claire Parnet convincingly argue, in that regard, that the 'becoming' of the United States was 'geographical', not least because 'American literature operates according to geographical lines: the flight towards the West, the discovery that the true East is in the West, the sense of the frontiers as something to cross, to push back, to go beyond'.[4]

Several recent studies have clearly demonstrated that 'American' literature was implicated in, and infused with, the imperial domination of foreign lands.[5] There is plenty of evidence on the Whitened narrative about the meaning of America: For instance, in his bestselling pamphlet *Common*

The myth of good AI

Sense, written during the American Revolution, Thomas Paine (1737–1809) equated the 'cause of America' to 'the cause of all mankind'. Of course, the myth of 'Anglo-Saxon' supremacy did not stand unopposed. Writers such as Herman Melville (1819–1891), who authored *Moby Dick*", and his contemporary Mark Twain (1835–1910), who created the characters Tom Sawyer and Huckleberry Finn, were very critical of the notion that America was somehow endowed with the mandate to create a world in its own Whitened image. Melville, in particular, used his unique talent to ridicule some of the imperialist tropes with parodical vigour. He criticised the mantra that 'the free can't conquer but to save', and that 'Americans are the peculiar, chosen people—the Israel of [the] time' that is destined to 'bear the ark of the liberties of the world' and made fun of the notion that the country always portrayed its actions in terms of 'national selflessness' and 'unbounded philanthropy' as 'the advance-guard', and that it failed to do 'a good to America' while it promised everything to the world.[6]

While this counter-culture continued to produce eloquent and outspoken dissent, successive US governments adhered to and reemphasised the idea that America is exceptional. This notion has been used as a ready-made formula to govern US society and to expand the class interest of the elites around the world. 'I always consider the settlement of America with reverence and wonder', wrote John Adams quite typically, eleven years before the Declaration of Independence in 1776, adding that he saw it 'as the opening of a grand scene in Providence for the illumination of the ignorant, and the emancipation of the slavish part of mankind all over the earth'.[7] The racist tropes of this discourse were clearly adopted from the European imperialists that we have already grappled with, as there was an emphasis on Americans being the 'chosen people' and therefore destined to rule the world. In the United States, as in Europe earlier, the imperial discourse was reliant on a crude self-designation based on (White) America's presumed racial and civilisational superiority. Such inherited, quintessentially European-Enlightenment attitudes are exemplified in the following speech by Republican Senator Albert Beveridge (1862–1927) in front of the US Senate in 1900. The quote serves as an adequate signpost to a deeper discussion of the political functionality of racism for the White-American narrative:

> The Philippines are ours forever, "territory belonging to the United States," as the Constitution calls them. And just beyond the Philippines are China's illimitable markets. ... We will not renounce our part in the mission of our race, trustee, under God, of the civilisation of the world. We will move forward to our work, not howling our regrets like slaves whipped to their burdens, but with gratitude for a task worthy of our strength, and thanksgiving to Almighty God that He has marked us as His chosen people, henceforth to lead in the regeneration of the world. ... Mr. President, this question is deeper than any question of party politics; deeper than any question of the isolated policy of our country even; deeper even than any question of constitutional power. It is elemental. It is racial. God has been preparing the English-speaking and Teutonic peoples for a thousand years for nothing but vain and idle self-contemplation and self-admiration. No! He has made us the master organisers of the world.[8]

The ideas of Beveridge about what it means to be American are not at all exceptional, of course. They did not develop in isolation. They travelled from Europe where ethnological race theories were professionalised at least from the eighteenth century onwards. The functionality of racism during the

Philippine-American War (1899–1903), which gives the quote from Beveridge its historical context, is picked up by several scholars. Meg Wesling emphasises the way racist tropes were incorporated into educational institutions, which strengthens our argument that we are grappling with bad data at the rhizomes of the so-called sciences and their institutional infrastructure. Wesling shows in great detail that the politics of Beveridge were by no means an isolated exception. This type of view was structural and systematically taught as an 'ameliorative and powerful force in the formation of citizens and the submission of colonial subjects'. In this project to stratify national and international society in accordance with the preferences of White Anglo-Saxons, education became an 'effective means of managing or "rehabilitating" racialized subjects — immigrants, African Americans, Native Americans, and Filipinos alike'.[9]

Other scholars have tackled similar issues from a different angle. For instance, Roxanne Lynn Doty focused on the emerging dichotomy between a Whitened west and the racialised non-west.[10] To that end, Filipinos were likened to the 'Negro', the 'Chinaman', the 'Indian', 'Mohammedan' and other 'coloured' and 'spotted' peoples deemed 'uncivilised' and racially 'inferior'.[11]

Doty's study is a good example for what we have called eugenicist geopolitics as she demonstrates the ordering of the Philippine-American War in accordance with the penumbra of racism. During the heyday of the Enlightenment, racism functioned as an ordering device to ensure the supremacy of the imperial classes over the rest. The primitive and primordial emphasis on the purity of blood legitimated the systematic subjugation of the African-American community, Native Americans and any other 'deviant' group in America itself (after all, slavery was written

Eugenic racism

into the Constitution of the United States). American racism has not only worked as a ready-made formula to subjugate various 'others' within US society. Being White secured a distinct form of politico-judicious sovereignty and privilege that was meant to structure both the domestic and international realms in favour of America's White immigrant elites from Europe.

The argument that I am furthering here is that at least since the eighteenth century, the idea of racial superiority was continuously inscribed into the American narrative, that it became a major trope in the self-perception of the emergent United States and that the theory of racial superiority expanded outwards from Enlightenment Europe. While the British strand of eugenics advocated by Sir Francis Galton (1822–1911) 'encouraged planned breeding of elites for their "noble qualities"', in North America 'eugenic practitioners quickly turned their attention to eliminating what they saw as negative characteristics of the poor: low intelligence, criminality, and unrestricted sexuality'.[12] Thus, the geo-ethnic invention that ordered the national narrative in North America at least since the eighteenth century was exported and reified through the thematic of White supremacy, which indicates the truly functional, eugenic biopower that racism unleashes, not only within the regimented contours of the nation and in international relations, but also in the rather more unstructured body of our virtual AI world, as we will establish in the second part of this chapter.

The fact that some of these tropes are recycled by right-wing movements, today should alert us to the salience of the bad data out there. Our archives are polluted. The battle against the 'other' continues with a ferocity comparable to the past, as the language of Donald Trump clearly demonstrates. When he alleged that some immigrants are 'poisoning the blood' of the

United States.[13] When he likened immigrants to 'rough people in many cases from jails, prisons, from mental institutions, insane asylums. You know, insane asylums – that's *Silence of the Lambs* stuff.' And when he said that 'we will use the best technology, including above and below ground sensors. That's the tunnels. … Towers, aerial surveillance and manpower',[14] then he clearly thinks in terms of that longstanding, subliminal supremacy complex of White America. This unculture is feeding into divisive AI algorithms that are magnified by right-wing influencers on social media websites, as we will continue to argue along the way.

Scholars and activists dealing with immigration should focus their attention on such abhorrent manifestations of racism today. Racism does not only have a material foundation, as Eduardo Bonilla-Silva argued in his important study. Racism is not only '*socially real*, boosted by the racial structures and practices of a racial order, and reenacted in the everyday life through encounters in all sorts of situations and spaces'.[15] In fact, the Enlightenment turned racism into both an imperial strategy and an ordering device within society with real 'scientific' pretensions. These bad legacies harboured in our archives, disciplines and institutions need to be reemphasised in order to establish a viable starting point for any discussion about the ethics of AI in our contemporary age. The following paragraphs will add to this dimension of our argument.

Racist medical algorithms

We have demonstrated that racism as a science was a distinct invention of the European Enlightenment and western modernity more generally and that it has been instrumental in ordering (national and international) society. In laboratories stacked

Eugenic racism

with skulls of homo sapiens, the idea was concocted that the (heterosexual) 'White Man' was destined to save humanity from the barbarism of the inferior races. The political manifestations are clear, and the rest of this chapter will set out how the new forms of eugenicist geopolitics are translated into a form of medical racism that continues to hamper AI applications in sensitive areas of society such as the health-care sector to this day.

This change of gear will support our argument that the Enlightenment created several predicaments that continue to cast a dark shadow on our age of Artificial Intelligence, and not only in politics, but also in sectors where you would least expect it, such as health care. For instance, at the time when Republican US Senators were advocating the eugenic ordering of the world, James Marion Sims, a nineteenth-century surgeon widely considered to be one of the founders of modern gynaecology, was experimenting with a treatment for vesicovaginal fistulas, a condition that affects bladder control and fertility in women. In his experiments between 1845 and 1849, Sims carried out surgeries on a dozen enslaved women without using any anaesthetic. He believed the then-common misconception that Black people could endure more pain than White people. This view still persists in the field of medicine and feeds into the data of AI algorithms. For example, comprehensive research has shown that a prominent health-care algorithm that determines which patients need more medical attention favoured White patients over Black patients whose condition was worse and who had more severe chronic health issues.[16] Indeed, early in 2023, a British MP authored a Women and Equalities Committee report which determined that racism is a major cause of massively higher maternal death rates among Black and disadvantaged women in the United Kingdom.[17]

The idea that Black patients have a higher pain threshold, then, is rooted in the tainted data that we inherited from the Enlightenment. Further research shows that White employees in the health-care sector are less likely to believe reports of pain by Black patients and therefore less likely to give them appropriate pain relief, in comparison to White patients with a comparable condition.[18] Another study by the Centers for Disease Control and Administration in the United States investigated the medical records of nearly 57,000 adults who had surgery between 2016 and 2021. It found that people of colour were 29% less likely to get regional anaesthesia in comparison to White patients.[19]

I have argued throughout this study that the starting point for programming rather more ethical AI algorithms has to be a better understanding of the polluted data enshrined in the edifices of our archives. We have to understand that in the birthplaces of western modernity, and certainly also in the United States as established above, medicine evolved in close conjunction with the 'science' of racism that we set out in the first part of this chapter. In particular, Native American and African-American women were victims of that insidious nexus between medical practice and racist abuse. Therefore, in the early twentieth century the eugenics movement that emerged in the United States adopted a favoured policy of European empires, as US eugenicists institutionalised compulsory sterilisation both in the legal statutes of the country and as a practice in the medical sector (e.g. the infamous Buck v. Bell case).[20]

Sterilisation of conquered and Indigenous populations was a major tool of colonialists, in order to control the population count in favour of the White immigrants and/or to ghettoise the Indigenous peoples. In Puerto Rico, sterilisation was introduced

Eugenic racism

by the Spanish colonialists. The practice was copied by the US in the form of the first 'birth control' organisation in Puerto Rico, established in 1925. At the same time in California, the US eugenicist Harry Laughlin drafted a law that would serve as a blueprint for the sterilisation laws of the Nazis in Germany. In thrall to eugenics, the US Congress enacted several laws designed to prevent immigration by Italians, Jews and other groups thought to be genetically inferior. In other settler-colonial settings such as Peru, Canada, Australia and Brazil, mass sterilisation campaigns were forcibly implemented in order to tip the demographic scale in favour of the White colonialists. Shockingly, this practice continues today.[21]

The historical examples of medical racism are manifold: In the nineteenth and early twentieth centuries in the United Kingdom, the United States and elsewhere, so-called 'resurrectionists' would be employed by medical schools to exhume the bodies of mostly subjugated 'coloured' people for medical examination and experimentation.[22] The aforementioned founder of gynaecology in the United States, James Marion Sims, 'came to many of his discoveries in the 19th century by experimenting on enslaved women, while also forcing them to perform domestic duties and serve as nurses in his clinic'.[23] In 1972, it was revealed that the United States Public Health Service had withheld syphilis treatment from hundreds of Black men who participated in a 40-year study observing the trajectory of the disease. The subjects of that experiment were mostly sharecroppers from rural Alabama 'whose informed consent was not collected'.[24] They were left under the impression that they had been treated for 'bad blood', a colloquial reference used at the time 'for several ailments, including syphilis, anemia, and fatigue'.[25] Instead of receiving proper treatment, they were given placebos, even after penicillin emerged as an effective antidote to syphilis in 1943. When considering that Black populations in the United States and the United Kingdom were wary about the COVID-19 vaccines leading to higher death rates relative to Whites, this history needs to be taken into account. It certainly should be discussed at every 'good AI' board meeting dealing with the medical sector.

The so-called Tuskegee study that denied the subjects that syphilis treatment was initiated in 1932 by Dr J.R. Heller at a time when racism was celebrated as a science in North America and Europe. The crucial point is that the 'study' was developed in order to test the common idea suggested by racism that Black people are biologically different to White people and that venereal diseases would therefore develop differently among them. When Hitler came to power in 1933, several professorships were endowed at German universities that furthered the racist idea of human 'perfection', most infamously at the University of Kiel in the northern state of Schleswig-Holstein. Henceforth, university professors' anthropological 'fieldwork' would include measuring the craniums of children as part of their medical investigations into phrenology and in order to establish if those children could be categorised as 'Aryan'. In all of these settings, medical racism enabled the theft, anatomical abuse and cruel display of bodies mostly of people of colour.

Today, the legacies of medical 'categorisation practices' furthered by eugenics and phrenology manifest themselves in biased and inaccurate AI algorithms. I have talked about some of these examples in *Is Artificial Intelligence Racist?* For instance, the American Civil Liberties Union established that facial recognition software such as Amazon's Rekognition tends to be racially biased, as 28 members of the US Congress, mostly non-White, were mistakenly matched with mugshot images of criminals.[26] Other software is similarly infected by bad algorithms, as dozens of Black Uber drivers have been repeatedly filtered out of the workforce because of what they indict as racist facial verification technology which fails to confirm their identity. Precariat workers are particularly affected by such biased software, which may explain why some of the tech-giants, certainly Amazon, are so adamantly opposed to unions. Despite the fact that some of these difficulties recognising the skin complexions of historically marginalised people persist, such facial recognition software continues to be aggressively marketed, not only to security organisations in the United States, but also to the medical sector where it is used in a range of health-care domains, from diagnosing diseases and conditions to so-called 'emotion detection' in mental-health therapies.

Part of the problem is the lack of diversity in the medical data as the nefarious historical legacies summarised above beget widespread mistrust of the health-care sector by minorities who tend to be more hesitant to volunteer for medical trials.[27] As a result, we are literally dealing with 'whitewashed' algorithmic data. Another example of the links between a polluted past and a problematic present that I flagged in previous studies: Despite the fact that fair-skinned people are at the highest risk of contracting skin cancer, the mortality rate for African-Americans is considerably higher, largely because of a lack of experience of diagnosing skin conditions in these historically marginalised strata of society, as the Association of American Medical Colleges establishes.[28] Therefore, melanoma for Black patients may be left untreated for longer than when it's diagnosed for patients categorised as White.

The myth of good AI

Transversal algorithms

AI-based technology has already shown that it has the potential to disrupt the social order beyond the medical sector.[29] Moreover, given the self-improving nature of the technology, which is incomparable to anything we have encountered before, AI is the only advance in world history that may do away with human supervision and control, as indicated in the introduction to this study. The so-called tech-giants are at the centre of the problem. The mission statements that their companies adhere to have a problematic 'colonial impulse', i.e. their agenda is all about expansion and therefore links up neatly with the imperial mentality that I dissected above. It is just that this type of expansion is different to previous forms in that it targets more than physical territory. Instead, it usurps our personal space and penetrates our bodies like no other technology before.

In fact, AI-driven eugenicist geopolitics is already upon us. Consider Elon Musk's aforementioned new company Neuralink. As I am writing these cautionary lines, Neuralink is developing brain-computer interfaces which are implanted by a so-called 'surgical robot'. This research area, too, is progressing with staggering speed and little oversight, as 'biochips and implants are built in new and better materials that produce no tissue rejection, incorporating nanotechnologies to diminish the size and with more powerful software to control and interact with the neural system'.[30] Neuroimplants harbour the possibility of 'controlling an individual's mental functions via wireless waves interacting with the electric activity of the brain'.[31] While companies such as MindMaze advertise such 'cognichips' as an option to rehabilitate individuals who have suffered from brain damage,[32] we will find out in chapter 4 how this technology will determine the future of torture.

Eugenic racism

Innovations like this continue the long and tragic tradition of mind control, by adding psychotic hallucinations to the frightening set of contemporary and future interrogation techniques.[33] The colonisation of our minds and bodies spearheaded by such human-AI interfaces must be understood as an extension of several Enlightenment legacies, in particular an obsession with biopolitical expansion and control which was central to cod sciences such as phrenology and eugenics. Here, the fact that Elon Musk has voiced his support for extremist right-wing parties such as the German *Alternative für Deutschland* (AFD),[34] which has openly expressed racist ideas and cultivates ties with neo-Nazi movements,[35] should alert us to the profound dangers of this nexus between politics and AI applications, especially in the medical and psycho-therapeutical sectors, as indicated. More recently, Musk has become one of the most vocal supporters of Donald Trump and part of his administration in a visible display of techno-power politics.

Bad data produce bad AI algorithms. If AI remains largely unchecked and unregulated, it will further entrench xenophobia and discrimination, especially where we can least afford it, such as in the medical sector. But there is hope. Once we trace and understand the historical roots of our polluted data, especially in Europe, Canada, Australia and North America, we can try to connect some of the problems of the past to solutions for the future, with particular reference to global institutions and civil society activism. This view was echoed by the House of Lords in the United Kingdom, which urged that the 'prejudices of the past must not be unwittingly built into automated systems, and such systems must be carefully designed from the beginning'.[36] While the House of Lords report cautioned against over-regulation, the World Health Organization (WHO) clearly (and rightly) prioritises setting global standards. According to the WHO, in order 'to protect human autonomy' and to ensure 'privacy and confidentiality', we need to provide 'patients with valid informed consent through appropriate legal frameworks'.[37] Other global institutions have identified the problem as well. In 2019, a major conference organised by UNESCO in Sao Paulo calibrated a response from Latin America and the Caribbean echoing a humanistic approach to AI technology and its usage, in particular in the medical sector.[38] One of the key policy take-aways of these efforts has been to ensure, even at this early stage, that AI applications remain under human supervision and that the onset of AGI – celebrated by posthumanists as the moment of Singularity when machines can think and act autonomously – does not yield a domino effect that removes human agency.

All the reports that have been surveyed for the present study clearly show that proper representation in research and data collection has a positive impact on policymaking, as the ethnicity data held by medical and other institutions are prone to bias. There are established ways to move beyond the bad legacies of the Enlightenment, suggested by concerned scholars. If divided spaces are the problem, as eugenics and phrenology were all about dividing and ruling peoples and bodies, then interpenetration of these artificially cleansed sectors of society must be the solution. This is not just a matter of proper representation of historically marginalised people, and gender balance. What we need in every 'good AI' board meeting is a dissident, who is well versed in ethical concepts from all over the world. He or she would curate ethical principles around inclusivity and a holistic appreciation of life and nature, as we laid out in the previous chapter.

Eugenic racism

Representation and criticism of established untruths have real practical benefits as they ensure that AI algorithms and corresponding datasets are auditable in accordance with communal, national and international human-rights legislation. In turn this inclusive and transparent approach will be helpful in safeguarding our most fundamental privacy rights, especially in the health-care sector, when AI applications are used during screening, diagnosis and treatment, and in ensuring that the results are clinically explainable to the patient throughout the medical process. In short, AI developers must be persuaded to ensure transparency and inclusivity, and utilise ethical standards codified by human-rights institutions. We must make them document their methods and results. If we don't confront them to that end, they will continue to think only in their deceptive bubble. Here, as everywhere else, then, we need more dialogue, more representation and above all better education and knowledge. As Kannin Osei-Tutu rightly argues in an important paper:

> Transformative change in medical education and practice demands explicit integration of anti-oppressive competencies. This shift aims to redefine the physician's role, moving from a neutral to an action-oriented stance committed to equity, justice, and addressing health disparities. ... Progress hinges on cultivating a critical mass of physicians committed to this change, thus paving the way for more equitable and just health care. ... By adopting an intersectional lens, this model expects physicians to recognize and challenge the ways in which various forms of oppression contribute to health inequities and strive for more inclusive care. All people ought to be treated as equal in dignity, but not all people are treated equally.[39]

There are further formulas in the better archives of the social sciences and the humanities that we can draw on in the debate about AI, despite their differing subject matter. For instance, John Hobson's proposition that Eurocentrism does not merely take the form of feting western culture, technology or politics and relegating non-western phenomena to 'deviances of *the* model' is useful to further this idea that we need hybrid spaces to ensure better datasets.[40] According to him, critical approaches from the left get caught in the Eurocentric trap as well, as they often depart from a core-periphery differentiation of the international system, which runs the risk of assuming that the west continuously determines events in the rest of the world. While it is prudent to appreciate the impact of 'neo-imperial' foreign policies and hegemonic systems, many scholars have stressed the multiplicity of linkages among multiple worlds that defy unidirectional power relations.[41] This attitude is clearly reflected in the hopeful political discourse in central regions of the Global South, such as South America. As it was proclaimed at the conference for sustainable development of AI in Latin America which ushered in a comprehensive Latin American Artificial Intelligence Index comprising a common strategy for research into and development of AI technology:

> When we look at challenges related to regulation or public policy development, and we do so with a multilateral perspective, what we achieve are international standards that help technology to be developed in a good way and ensure that the values underpinning that technological development are shared by countries and nations with similar thinking. And that is a great contribution of this community with regard to science and technology ... We are sure that the first Latin American Artificial Intelligence Index will be a tremendous contribution to public policy development, which will join the shared efforts that many of our countries in Latin America and the Caribbean are making.[42]

The language and research design of such nascent approaches challenge the overwhelmingly positivist value placed on western power. Setting such strategic signposts for the future does not call for substituting 'westernism' with 'easternism', but it requires analyses of the hybrid fields of intercultural engagement endowed in global history, which offer an opportunity to capture a common human narrative. This is particularly important within politico-cultural contexts where there is an emphasis on justice and equality, such as in the discourse of 'good AI'. In this way, critical AI studies could thrive in the absence of an obligation to centre Artificial Intelligence geographically or culturally or to reinvigorate ideational markers that reproduce the myth of primordial, all-encompassing and insurmountable differences between 'us' and 'them'. Only in this way can we envision a future freed from the shackles of our insidious past.

Notes

1 See among others Safiya Umoja Noble, *Algorithms of Oppression: How search engines reinforce racism*, New York: New York University Press, 2018.
2 Lloyd Strickland and Jia Wang, 'Racism and Eurocentrism in Histories of Philosophy', *Open Journal of Philosophy*, Vol. 13 (2023), pp. 76–96.
3 See Michael Hardt and Antonio Negri, *Multitude: War and democracy in the age of empire*, London: Penguin, 2004, p. 313.
4 Gilles Deleuze and Claire Parnet, 'On the Superiority of Anglo-American Literature', in Gilles Deleuze and Claire Parnet (eds.), *Dialogues II*, trans. Hugh Tomlinson, Barbara Habberjam, New York: Columbia University Press, 2007, p. 37.
5 See in particular Ryan's work on US foreign policy, for instance, David Ryan, *US Foreign Policy in World History*, London: Routledge, 2000 and Michael Patrick Cullinane and David Ryan (eds.), US Foreign Policy and the Other, London: Berghahn Books, 2014. On the nexus

between imperialism and US literature, see Meg Wesling, *Empire's Proxy: American literature and U.S. imperialism in the Philippines*, New York: New York University Press, 2011.

6   Herman Melville, *Redburn His First Voyage – White Jacket or The World in a Man-of-War – Moby-Dick or, The Whale*, New York: The Library of America, 1983, p. 506.

7   Quoted in James Chace, *The Consequences of the Peace: The new internationalism and American foreign policy*, Oxford: Oxford University Press, 1992, pp. 170–171.

8   *Congressional Record*, 56th Congress, 1st session, 1900, 33, pt. 1, pp. 704, 710–711.

9   Wesling, *Empire's Proxy*, p. 3.

10 Roxanne Lynn Doty, *Imperial Encounters: The politics of representation in North-South relations*, London: University of Minnesota Press, 1996, p. 33.

11 *Ibid.*, p. 43.

12 Virginia Eubanks, *Automating Inequality: How high-tech tools profile, police, and punish the poor*, London: Picador, 2019, p. 22.

13 'What Did Trump Say? Explaining the former president's favourite talking points', NPR, 11 May 2024. Available at www.npr.org/2024/05/11/1245900177/trump-rally-speech-talking-points-rhetoric-immigration-abortion accessed 12 June 2024.

14 'Transcript of Donald Trump's immigration speech', *New York Times*, 1 September 2016. Available at www.nytimes.com/2016/09/02/us/politics/transcript-trump-immigration-speech.html accessed 12 June 2024.

15 Eduardo Bonilla-Silva, *Racism without Racists: Colour-blind racism and the persistence of racial inequality in America*, London: Rowman & Littlefield, 2022, p. 21 (emphasis in the original).

16 See Ziad Obermeyer, Brian Powers, Christine Vogeli and Sendhil Mullainathan, 'Dissecting Racial Bias in an Algorithm Used to Manage the Health of Populations', *Science*, Vol. 366, No. 6464 (2019), pp. 447–453.

17 House of Commons Women and Equalities Committee, *Black Maternal Health Third Report of Session 2022–23 Report, together with formal minutes relating to the report*, 18 April 2023. Available at https://committees.parliament.uk/publications/38989/documents/191706/default/ accessed 12 December 2023.

18 Kelly M. Hoffman, Sophie Trawalter, Jordan R. Axt and M. Norman Oliver, 'Racial Bias in Pain Assessment and Treatment

Recommendations, and False Beliefs about Biological Differences between Blacks and Whites', *Procedures of the National Academy of Sciences, USA*, Vol. 113, No. 19 (2019), pp. 4296–4301.

19 See Tina Reed, 'CDC: Maternal mortality disparities have worsened', *Axios*, 23 February 2022. Available at www.axios.com/2022/02/23/us-maternal-mortality-disparities-by-race accessed 6 February 2023.

20 See Paolo Alonso, 'Autonomy Revoked: The forced sterilization of women of color in 20th century America'. Available at https://twu.edu/media/documents/history-government/Autonomy-Revoked--The-Forced-Sterilization-of-Women-of-Color-in-20th-Century-America.pdf accessed 6 January 2023.

21 Gillian Rutherford, 'Reproductive control of Indigenous women continues around the world, say survivors and researchers', *Folio*, 27 June 2022. Available at www.ualberta.ca/folio/2022/06/reproductive-control-of-indigenous-women-continues-around-the-world.html accessed 2 March 2023.

22 See Ayah Nuriddin, Graham Mooney and Alexandre White, 'The Art of Medicine: Reckoning with histories of medical racism and violence in the USA', *The Lancet*, Vol. 396, No. 10256 (2020), pp. 949–951.

23 *Ibid.*

24 US Department of Health & Human Services, 'The U.S. Public Health Service Untreated Syphilis Study at Tuskegee', no date. Available at www.cdc.gov/tuskegee/about/timeline.html?CDC_AAref_Val=https://www.cdc.gov/tuskegee/timeline.htm accessed 10 December 2024.

25 *Ibid.*

26 See Jacob Snow, 'Amazon's Face Recognition Falsely Matched 28 Members of Congress With Mugshots', American Civil Liberties Union, 26 July 2018. Available at www.aclu.org/news/privacy-technology/amazons-face-recognition-falsely-matched-28 accessed 2 January 2022.

27 See Amy Schulz, Cleopatra Caldwell and Sarah Foster, '"What Are They Going to Do With the Information?" Latino/Latina and African American Perspectives on the Human Genome Project', *Health Education & Behaviour*, Vol. 30, No. 2 (2003), pp. 151–169.

28 'Why Are So Many Black Patients Dying of Skin Cancer?', Association of American Medical Colleges, 21 July 2022. Available at www.aamc.org/news/why-are-so-many-black-patients-dying-skin-cancer accessed 12 June 2024.

29 For more, see Adib-Moghaddam, *Is Artificial Intelligence Racist?*, 2023.
30 Pau Pérez-Sales, 'The Future is Here: Mind control and torture in the digital era', *Torture: Quarterly Journal on Rehabilitation of Torture Victims and Prevention of Torture*, Vol. 32, No. 1–2, pp. 280–290 (p. 284).
31 *Ibid.*, p. 284
32 See 'The Struggle to Create a Microchip that Can Mimic the Human Brain and Open a Portal to Another World', MindMaze, 20 June 2018. Available at https://mindmaze.com/the-struggle-to-create-a-microchip-that-can-mimic-the-human-brain/ accessed 25 December 2023.
33 See also Armin Krishnan, *Military Neuroscience and the Coming Age of Neurowarfare*, London: Routledge, 2016.
34 Charles R. Davis, 'Elon Musk attacked German support for migrants and promoted a call to support a far-right extremist political party', *Business Insider*, 29 September 2023. Available at www.businessinsider.com/elon-musk-immigration-migrants-germany-far-right-extremism-twitter-x-2023-9 accessed 10 December 2023.
35 'Rassistisch und Rechtsextrem: Klare Abgrenzung von der AfD Geboten', Deutsches Institut für Menschenrechte, 7 June 2021. Available at www.institut-fuer-menschenrechte.de/aktuelles/detail/rassistisch-und-rechtsextrem-klare-abgrenzung-von-der-afd-geboten accessed 1 December 2023.
36 House of Lords, *AI in the UK: ready, willing and able? – Government response to the select committee report. Report of session 2017–19*, 16 April 2017, p. 5
37 United Nations, 'WHO guidance on Artificial Intelligence to improve healthcare, mitigate risks worldwide', *UN News*, 28 June 2021. Available at https://news.un.org/en/story/2021/06/1094902 accessed 12 July 2022.
38 'UNESCO Promotes a Human-Rights Based Approach to AI Development during the Regional Forum on AI in Latin America and the Caribbean', UNESCO, 17 December 2019. Available at www.unesco.org/en/articles/unesco-promotes-human-rights-based-approach-ai-development-during-regional-forum-ai-latin-america accessed 18 December 2023.
39 Kannin Osei-Tutu, 'Redefining Excellence in Health Care: Uniting inclusive compassion and shared humanity within a transformative physician competency model', *Canadian Medical Association Journal (CMAJ)*, Vol. 196, No. 11 (2024), pp. E81–E83.

40 John Hobson, 'Is Critical Theory Always For the White West and For Western Imperialism? Beyond Westphilian towards a post-racist critical IR', *Review of International Studies*, Vol. 33 (2007), pp. 91–116 (p. 93 – emphasis in the original).
41 Pinar Bilgin, 'Thinking Past "Western" IR?', *Third World Quarterly*, Vol. 29, No. 1 (2008), pp. 5–23 (p. 6).
42 'Artificial Intelligence Can Contribute to Transforming Development Models in Latin America and the Caribbean to Make Them More Productive, Inclusive and Sustainable', ECLAC – United Nations, 11 August 2023. Available at www.cepal.org/en/pressreleases/artificial-intelligence-can-contribute-transforming-development-models-latin-america accessed 6 December 2023.

3
Techno-Orientalism

Let's situate ourselves. We have pointed out that the 'west', assumed to be quintessentially superior, received significant input from the 'east'.[1] Indeed, the previous chapters showed how the east has actually contributed to the ideational and material constitution of the west (the same applies to the south/north dialectic). More critically attuned scholarship experiments quite fruitfully with concepts beyond the west, applying those to empirical examples in Europe and North America in order to unravel Eurocentric assumptions. These studies navigate the zone where geography and transcultural/transidentitarian factors trouble each other, where there is an appreciation that poverty within Detroit's 8 Mile is felt in a comparable way to Cairo's poverty-stricken districts; that youth gangs in South Central Los Angeles have more in common with their counterparts in Cape Town than with people living on the other side of LA in Beverly Hills, whose lives may be rather more akin to those of the citizens of San Isidro in Lima, Peru.[2] These transversal connections could direct the emergent discipline of critical AI studies toward the limits of coherence across geography, civilisation, identity, culture and race. In essence, programmers of AI systems have to consider that race is a social construction – there is no such thing as a primordially defined difference between White and Black or any other such invented category. The starting point for AI ethics has to be our common humanity.

To that end, putting emphasis on the entangled history of subjects and collectives on a truly global scale does not deny the persistence of antagonistic differences, or forms of disjunctive syntheses. Recent scholarship has made great strides toward appreciating the zones of convergence and conflict between local developments and global factors, specific ideational trends and general trans-identitarian movements, between sub-national divergence, national disintegration and transnational loyalty.[3] Pinar Bilgin, for instance, proposes to trace difference through investigating the 'emergence of ways of thinking and doing the same but not quite'.[4] As an emergent theme in critical theory, the appreciation of difference within a common human experience has offered an important route away from the deceptive promise of 'identity' and it can be fixed here as a major prerequisite for truly 'good AI'.

Difference within a common, globally experienced universality can be pinned down further with reference to recent upheavals in the name of a common humanity, certainly the Arab Spring in 2011. The uprisings which started in Tunisia and spread like wildfire on both sides of the Mediterranean to Egypt, Libya, Greece, Spain and further afield revealed a dual tendency, a paradox if you wish. On the one side, such emancipative movements point to the process of hybridisation, the breakdown of grand narratives and ideational systems in an increasingly networked, postmodernised order, where ideational factors such as religious affiliation and nationality play a secondary role. The Arab Spring was indicative of this post-ideological and trans-ideational world. The demonstrations were inspired by universal ideas such as democracy, social justice, empowerment and pluralism. At the same time they were local, steeped in the secular and Muslim symbols and imagery that permeate the societies of Tunisia, Egypt and elsewhere. It has been a misjudgement of Eurocentric theories of globalisation to assume that 'the local' will dissolve in the great stream of 'the global', a mantra that AI strategists adhere to as well. Rather, globality and locality are increasingly intermingled and inseparable. The properties of both are being changed in a grand dialectical firework.[5]

If 'ensuring inclusion in the AI world' is the aim, as professed by the Global Forum on the Ethics of Artificial Intelligence hosted by the Czech Presidency of the Council of the EU in December 2022,[6] then we need to start with a fundamental acknowledgement that the mythical stories about origin, and the almost sacrosanct service they supply to imperial power, continue to be a root cause of many conflicts on a global scale. In Europe, confrontational ideologues with access to government fan the flames of Islamophobia, giving new life to the psycho-nationalist politics of exclusion, sometimes with insidiously racist undertones. In Hungary, Italy, Austria, Sweden, Germany, France and Britain, the exclusionary agendas of right-wing parties have gained a foothold among mainstream politicians, as they dominate a range of problematic narratives on social media sites. Terrorists such as Anders Breivik in Norway, who was responsible for the murder of dozens of teenagers in 2011, or neo-Nazi movements in Germany, who organised and executed the systematic killing of immigrant workers and advocate vile antisemitism, defy politics and position themselves explicitly against the state, summoning their supporters into a new dawn of fascism. Decentralised terrorist movements such as al-Qaeda or ISIS and their sympathisers are equally adamant about reminding their constituencies online that they are killing in the name of a higher ideal. Contemporary terrorism feeds on the fertile ground of exclusionary identity politics. The symbols, imagery and norms vary in accordance with local realities, but the mechanisms and political rationale behind the actions are largely comparable.

This chapter furthers our discussion of bad science and systems of untruth that feed into some of the bad data that are negatively affecting minorities and other vulnerable members of society. Critical scholars have introduced the term 'Techno-Orientalism' in order to shed some much-needed conceptual light on such forms of exclusion. In an important compilation of articles, some of these critical scholars link Techno-Orientalism to stereotypical representations of Asians and Asia itself as technologically adept, yet intellectually underdeveloped and therefore in need of western tutelage.[7] Traditional Orientalism depicted the peoples of the east as essentially backward because of their alleged racial inferiority. With the resurgence of Asian power centred around China, this attitude is very difficult to maintain. Therefore, traditional Orientalist attitudes have transmuted into depicting Asians as 'essentially robotic—automata capable of fine-tuned execution and coordination, but lacking the sort of individual creativity and spirit that defined the Western subject'.[8] In order to safeguard western dominance from the inevitable re-emergence of Asia as a locus for global power, a process of othering continues as the west represents 'platforms in China as something inferior, different, or even morally depraved. For example, WeChat,

The myth of good AI

Weibo, Baidu, and Alibaba have been colloquially made sense of within and outside China as resemblances or counterfeits of Facebook, Twitter, Google, and eBay/Amazon respectively.'[9] In the work of Wendy Hui Kyong Chun, the problem of such high-tech Orientalism is more profound. According to her, it safeguards a White hegemony over the definition of what it means to be human, reiterating a racial hierarchy that rationalises the exploitation of the 'other'. For Kyong Chun, we need a new form of critical posthumanism to counter such enforced demarcations and to challenge the racist hierarchies that are part of the human experience.[10]

Causes and effects of 'good AI'

The ordering of the fundamental human-non-human divide that Kyong Chun criticises as a breeding ground for Techno-Orientalism could only be achieved by dependence on uninhibited causality. The ordering of the age of Artificial Intelligence is no exception. In fact, the algorithmic logic at the heart of our current tech societies is absolutely dependent on speeding up if-then propositions in order to buttress hierarchies of power. This simulation of fantastic speed via infinitely galvanised causal conjunctions is another inheritance from the Enlightenment and its emphasis on de-historicised sequences that isolate an exclusive western temporality for the governing elites. It is in this way, that western man sought to detach himself from interdependence with others, thus effecting a separate status codified in racial terms as indicated. Any impingement from the 'outside' by immigrants or critical voices from the 'in-group' threatens that artificial encampment of western myth. If it is the case that 'highly accurate algorithmic predictions that non-accidentally correlate with race do so because the process successfully "learns" the social effects that racial distinctions have in the world and leverages these correlations in making predictions',[11] then it is true that we need a critical approach to race that battles with the bad data transmitted by our archives. If the 'social and political forces continually shape the boundaries of racial categories, their meanings, and as a result, their causal roles' and if 'racial divisions can only be maintained and produced anew by *race-making institutions*',[12] then delving into the way causal inferences are inscribed into those institutions should be central to 'good AI' and its emphasis on inclusive algorithms.

Here, as well, we need to look back in order to establish a better algorithmic syntax for the future. The extreme positivism of the Enlightenment that scholars such as Hayden White dissected is partially responsible for the current algorithmic belief in cleansed causal totalities.[13] Starting with Count Henri de Saint-Simon (1760–1825) and continued even more fervently by Auguste Comte (1798–1857), the vast majority of writers during the European Enlightenment had an almost fanatical trust in the merits of independent and 'objective' causation. It was this moment of intense controversy about the legitimate methods to explain human existence, Hayden White argues, which produced a conception of rationalism derived from the (Newtonian) physical sciences which assumed that truth and reality are free and independent of the (White) viewer and observer. Enlightenment philosophers conceptualised world history in terms of 'cause-effect relationships'. The binary thus created positioned 'enlightened Europe' in opposition to the 'ignorant' rest of the world. 'The "syntax" of relationships by which these two classes of historical phenomena were bound together was that of the unremitting conflict of opposites.'[14] In their beautifully intelligent classic, *Dialectic of Enlightenment* published in post-war Germany, Theodor Adorno and Max Horkheimer presaged the stupid fairytales that some of the 'good AI' proponents couch in 'positivist' language today. Their warning about blind belief in Enlightenment legacies sounds like an eerie premonition of our predicament with some of the narratives of 'good AI':

> The blindness and dumbness of the data to which positivism reduces the world pass over into language itself, which restricts itself to recording those data. Terms themselves become impenetrable; they obtain a striking force, a power of adhesion and repulsion which makes them like their extreme opposite, incantations. They come to be a kind of trick, because the name of the prima donna is cooked up in the studio on a statistical basis … The lack of concern for the subject makes things easy for administration. Ethnic groups are forced to move to a different region; individuals are branded as Jews and sent to the gas chamber.[15]

It should not come as a surprise to the educated reader, then, that the invention of causal inference as an exclusively western prerogative lent itself to Orientalism as yet another regime of untruth taught as a science at universities. In turn, this history explains why Techno-Orientalism is a problem for the AI world today. The treatment of the 'other' as object has been fundamentally in accord with the extreme arrogance of the causal imperative that is at the heart of the positivist promise which is now central to our AI algorithms as indicated. Taken to its logical end, AI is disseminating into our current world the discourse of the Enlightenment that everything was possible and, by implication that a particular breed of men had been granted the historical mandate to make it possible. Inevitably, to explain the 'other' became a strategy of showing that her essence can be deduced and hence predicted from scientific, observable and approachable natural laws. The thrust of these causal myths of the Enlightenment served not only to widen the cognitive framework for the Manichean allegories of previous centuries (Christianity v. Islam, barbarism v. the Greek polis, Aryan v. Semitic etc.), but to objectify them as scientific laws, as real, inevitable and primordial.

In the same manner, AI is sold to us as objective and 'unbiased'; as the new all-encompassing science of humanity. As one prominent tech observer remarked recently: 'To a large extent, the data scientists of today are like the monks of 2000 years ago, when they were literate but they didn't show other people how to write. ... It's like almost any religion where we have the leaders holding secrets, giving them power and authority. From my perspective as a mathematician, it is an abuse of this authority'.[16] As a result of this abuse, vulnerable and historically marginalised people continue to be invented as objects of technology, much in the same way as the Enlightenment predicated. Studying these historically marginalised people is not only made infinitely more possible by AI, but becomes a primary obsession of a range of technological sites of surveillance.[17] This continued emphasis on objectivity and visibility, which is central to the 'good AI' marketing ploy, by necessity of the positivistic premises thus inculcated, reifies a central dynamic of the current age of Artificial Intelligence: It reinscribes the power of the tech-giants into every algorithm governing our daily life, thus effecting a hierarchisation of society that is particularly oppressive for historically marginalised people and the economically destitute.

The myth of good AI

Musk(ism)

There is plenty of evidence to relocate our discussion of history to current social and political problems galvanised by the AI *zeitgeist*. Elon Musk emerges as a focal point here, as some of his actions and proclamations support our argument that there exists an insidious nexus between technology and various forms of extremism. As indicated, Musk has not only voiced his support for coup d'états against democratically elected presidents (namely Evo Morales in Bolivia) and extremist right-wing parties with neo-Nazi inclinations (i.e. the AFD in Germany), but his companies have repeatedly failed to curb various forms of racial abuse. Musk can't be held personally responsible for the racism endured by Owen Diaz and other Black workers at Tesla factories who were told to 'go back to Africa' and had to face racist graffiti and depictions in their workspace.[18] But the US Equal Employment Opportunity Commission, as well as the California Civil Rights Department *did* indict Tesla for widespread racist discrimination.[19] The latter argued that Black workers were kept 'in the lowest level roles in the company' and that they were paid less than White and other colleagues. Black workers were denied 'training and promotions'; they were 'disciplined … more severely than others' and their complaints about racial slurs 'were practically ignored', while Tesla remained 'unreasonably' slow in cleaning up '"racist graffiti with swastikas and other hate symbols scrawled in common areas"'.[20]

I am reiterating that Elon Musk can't be held responsible for every incident of racism in his factories. Neither do I deem him closely aligned to extremist agendas. Musk is interested in profit and he acts in accordance with his tech ideology. His actions are geared to those goals and to his limited world-view as a self-conscious White man who has never intimately studied radically different cultures. With reference to the case above, Tesla itself did indicate in its (rather lukewarm) responses that such problems were investigated and actions against the perpetrators were taken.[21]

However, one of the arguments of the present study has been that racism is an ordering device, in the sense that it legitimates and buttresses systems of domination. The fact that there are no Black executives at Tesla and that Black professionals seem seriously underrepresented corresponds to that argument. Furthermore, until the successful lawsuit brought forward by Owen Diaz, Tesla didn't even have any written charter or established procedures to address forms of discrimination or racial abuse affecting its employees at work.[22] Finally, it is not as if Musk has come out squarely against racism in his various public proclamations. Rather than addressing the issue of racism at his factories, he is on record as speaking of racism against Whites. He remarked on Twitter that unarmed White individuals affected by police violence do not get sufficient coverage in the media compared to Black people who are killed or injured by police. Musk argued that this media representation is 'Very disproportionate to promote a false narrative'.[23] He failed to add the statistical facts which prove him wrong: 'Black people are 3.5 times more likely than white people to be killed by police when Blacks are not attacking or do not have a weapon'.[24] Neither did Musk appreciate that 'Black teenagers are 21 times more likely than white teenagers to be killed by police'.[25] Our problems today, then, do have to do with bad data and relatively low levels of empathy and multicultural education among some of the leading figures of the tech world. Musk, for sure, is not known for his support for the poor strata of society or marginalised communities in the United States or elsewhere. Instead he chooses to support Donald Trump and the colonisation of Mars.

It is this general reluctance to acknowledge what I have called eugenicist geopolitics as a problem that complements our argument about the hierarchies of power that the AI *zeitgeist* aids and abets. Techno-Orientalism is part of that process of techno-othering. Certainly, Orientalism was always about legitimising expansion in the name of civilisation, always about empire as indicated. It was also about ordering society in favour of the imperial elites. The evidence shows that the actions of Elon Musk can be placed within that genealogy, also in terms of some his ideological allegiances. There are simply too many examples to choose from to support that angle of our analysis: For instance, as I am writing these lines, Musk has agreed with a Twitter post which shared images of predominantly North African immigrants arriving on the Italian island of Lampedusa. The post referred to the refugees as a 'George Soros-led invasion'. Musk responded that the 'Soros organization seems to want nothing less than the destruction of Western civilization', in a categorical tone similar to right-wing commentators.[26] It should be added that George Soros is a Holocaust survivor who has been the subject of numerous anti-Semitic conspiracy theories. His Open Science Foundation supports refugees through various aid mechanisms and funding schemes.[27] In another related and recent example, Musk professed a belief in cultural coherence and identity when he spoke at an event at the invitation of the right-wing President of Italy, Georgia Meloni. Musk made the case for 'more Italians' and against the seemingly divisive policies of the environmental movement and 'far left crazy people at US colleges'.[28] And perhaps Musk really doesn't know that Italy was only invented as a nation state in the nineteenth century and that it has always been a crossroads for different cultures and peoples.[29] The lack of historical education *is* a problem in the tech world.

Comparable to traditional Orientalism, institutionalised as science during the Enlightenment and immortalised in the canonical study of the late Edward Said,[30] Techno-Orientalism is always also about reinforcing boundaries between us and them, east and west, Black and White, and in the case of Musk's appearance in Italy, real Italians and inauthentic immigrants. A typical example was Samuel P. Huntington's infamous thesis of an inevitable clash of civilisations between Islam and the west, one of the most uninformed books ever written by a Harvard academic, which I dissected in my research over a decade ago.[31] Repeatedly, Musk uses comparably unnuanced and analytically false categories when he speaks of a threat to western civilisation from stranded immigrants from Africa, or emphasises 'humanity' when he talks about cultural authenticity at right-wing events. Language as a border-creating device – this is Enlightenment nonsense par excellence and it is exponentially magnified on social media sites.

Furthermore, since taking over Twitter (now called X), Musk has implemented a general amnesty for formerly banned users of the platform, reinstating thousands of accounts 'including neo-Nazis, white supremacists, misogynists and spreaders of dangerous conspiracy theories'.[32] Again, this may be a business decision as chaos, violence and destruction sell – deeper thoughts and ideas can't be expressed within the word limit on X or 'flicked' or 'reeled' on other social media platforms.[33] But it is also indicative of tolerance for various forms of extremism which are harmful to society and our democratic systems while singling out US college lecturers or environmentalists as particularly divisive, as indicated above. Ultimately, by changing its profit strategy to promoting posts by subscribed users, X feeds into a massive misinformation culture that galvanises the agenda of the right wing and opens the platform up to overt and covert influencers connected to extremist political agendas. Musk himself is a perpetrator, for example, when he proclaimed that 'civil war is inevitable' at the height of the violent riots throughout British cities in the summer of 2024, where mosques were attacked and historically marginalised people were beaten. Musk could have called for dialogue and reconciliation. Rather, he shared, and later on deleted, a false X post from the co-leader of the extremist Britain First party about the Labour government in Britain building 'detainment camps' for rioters.[34] No wonder then that the 'truth' can be bought on X and other social media platforms. No wonder also that all over the world extremists are connecting and organising online.

Musk himself is certainly not an extremist. He really seems to think that what he does is ethical and that he defends freedom of speech, with no real understanding that the freedom to pursue one's desires should not harm others. It is equally certain that some of his tech projects aid and abet extremism. In her important study pinpointing surveillance capitalism, Zuboff clearly established the link between the creation of extremist binaries and maximising the profit margins of the tech-giants. Tolerating extremism, in short, is considered to be an acceptable business model, as the Center for Countering Digital Hate estimated that the value of only 'ten reinstated accounts renowned for publishing hateful content and dangerous conspiracies will generate up to $19 million a year in advertising revenue for Twitter'.[35] This link between extremism and maximising profit margins may also explain why Musk came out against tempering the misogyny and racism of unfiltered large language models such as ChatGPT in the name of free speech. In that regard, a 'narrative appears to be developing in rightwing areas of the internet – now amplified by Musk – that racism and sexism are desirable features in AI'.[36]

Our research has demonstrated that Musk has repeatedly supported the causes of some of the most reactionary strata of society with his actions and words. One common theme can be deduced from all of this: For Musk, no matter the politics involved, the media attention means crisis situations are business opportunities to expand the profit margins of his companies. From this perspective, there is not much room for strategies geared to humanitarian aid, social emancipation or cultural empathy. It is in this way that 'Musk(ism)' is part of the problem. Its underlying ideological precepts are not meant to answer the appeals of vulnerable members of society who are chafing under the paternalistic surveillance of AI technology. How easily the word 'humanistic' disappears in this context and how easy it is to understand why, as the narcissistic egoism, divisiveness and capitalist megalomania of the age of Artificial Intelligence become clearer to us.

X imperialism and its discontents

(Techno-)Orientalism as an incubator of imperial expansion in order to maximise profits for a select few: When Elon Musk praises Chinese factory workers for not just 'burning the midnight oil [but] burning the 3am oil, they won't even leave the factory ... whereas in America people are trying to avoid going to work at all', he makes that transmission belt explicit.[37] This

The myth of good AI

type of hyper-capitalist mentality advocated by Musk and others has ushered in what one could call 'X imperialism'. X imperialism is literally extraterrestrial as it targets the universe as we know it. We know by now that its expansionist logic dates back to the age of the Enlightenment. Ideas such as 'occupying Mars', as Musk advocates, are all about colonisation. I fail to see the difference to the British imperialists advocating colonisation, which was criticised by the brilliant H. G. Wells in his tales of space colonies that take other people's land and oppress the 'natives'. The Peruvian intellectual Aníbal Quijano rightly termed this impulse the 'coloniality of power', a concept central to Latin American postcolonial studies and influential in North American decolonial approaches. The work of Quijano and his disciples acknowledges the legacies of European colonialism and their reification in social institutions and knowledge systems.[38] Today, X imperialism is proliferating in the digital world.

Musk shares with traditional imperialism a strange obsession with population control and a 'threat to the west' in that regard, which resembles some of the eugenicist geopolitical legacies outlined in the previous chapter.[39] Traditional imperialism aggrandised the idea of the west abusing science to create fiction, much in the same way as it is done today. For instance, the Mercator world map – upon which most world atlases for schools, airlines, catalogues, YouTube geographies and tourist guides were modelled – falsely inflates the landmass of the northern hemisphere. In actual fact, the size of the land in the southern hemisphere is twice that in the northern one. Yet on the Mercator, the landmass of the north covers two-thirds of the map while the landmass of the south is limited to only a third. So, for example, Scandinavia is allocated the same amount of space as India, although the former is in actual fact about a third of the size of the latter. China is dwarfed, too, as Greenland appears twice as big as China on the map. In reality, Greenland is about one-quarter of the size of China.[40]

The idea of limitless expansion, central to what I have called eugenicist geopolitics, is at the heart of Musk(ism), too. The key promise of colonial expansion has always been linked to the renewal of the motherland through the economic exploitation of newly conquered territories and their colonisation by settlers. The promises of Musk (and others) about the possibility and merits of colonising other planets is driven by a comparable imperial impulse. The science fiction of 'terraforming' Mars by dropping 'thermonuclear bombs over its poles', as Musk suggested,[41] connects quite directly to the mentality of Enlightenment colonialists who advocated expansion, rather than improving the conditions in their own societies. Extraterrestrial colonialism is offered here as an escape route from existential threats to our planet, creating the mirage that we can simply find new territories to settle in, rather than improving our conditions in the here and now. The activities of SpaceX, Musk's company that is at the heart of this X imperialism, follow the logic 'that there will be some extinction event. The alternative is to become a space-faring civilization and multi-planetary species', Musk suggested at the Sixty-Seventh International Astronautical Congress in 2016.[42]

In the same way that the colonial atrocities of the past were rationalised through tropes such as Orientalism or the racial superiority of the White race that were rendered scientific, today's X imperialism is premised on an ideology that represents current trends as inevitable and determined by natural laws that can't be resisted. Take a look at Musk's posts: They are all about inevitabilities, written with positivist conviction, but factually wrong most of the time. In this way, X imperialism makes possible a very particular epistemic privilege: It arrogates to a handful of men the luxury of interpreting, judging and planning the future for the majority.

In Musk and others, there is always this pathological, unnuanced, deceptively positivist emphasis on inevitabilities. There appears this mirage of the last 'step to objective knowledge of the historical world, which stands on a par with the knowledge of nature achieved by modern science'.[43] In terms of psychology, positivism of this kind can also be described as a particular form of patriarchal megalomania, which was a typical personality trait of the traditional imperialists: 'These stars that you see overhead at night, these vast worlds which we can never reach', Cecil Rhodes, one of the godfathers of nineteenth-century British imperialism famously said, 'I would annex the planets if I could. I often think of that.'[44] The lack of nuance and understanding of the plight of others is emblematic for such attitudes. Musk, as well, arrogates to himself the authority to override complexities in order to present himself as an intellectual visionary, even as a philosopher: 'My driving philosophy is to expand the scope and scale of consciousness that we may better understand the nature of the universe,' Musk establishes almost at a whim. 'I have a sort of proposal for a worldview or motivating philosophy which is to understand what questions to ask about the answer that is the universe'.[45] Musk did not finish his PhD. Neither did he study any of the social sciences or humanities. His ideas do not gain traction because they are informed by serious study and peer review, and refined through scholarly dialogues. They are out there because he has built his own institutions to proclaim them. X may make his ideas influential, but they remain untrue and largely primitive, not least by virtue of the limitations of the platform itself.

Where the power of such tech utopias are invoked, it is often in reaction to the disorder of our postmodern condition, which unsettles the safe territories carved out by the grand narratives of modernity, which have failed to deliver the promised utopias that constituted the tragedies of the twentieth century, namely Fascism and Communism. In our modern past, grand narratives were rather more successful in simulating order and giving a common sense of shared identity, which moulded the nation/civilisation/community into a seemingly coherent unit. The transversal movements of our current condition, which has created mixture, hybridity and difference, have unsettled the myth of cultural purity. It should not be forgotten that both neo-Nazi movements in Europe and ISIS terrorists kill in the name of sameness, the former with an emphasis on race and ethnicity, the latter from an obsession with religious separation. As Paul Gilroy pointed out in his beautiful indictment of the politics of exclusion:

> To have mixed is to have been party to a great betrayal. Any unsettling traces of hybridity must be excised from the tidy, bleached-out zones of impossibly pure culture. The safety of sameness can then be recovered by either of the two options that have regularly appeared at the meltdown point of this dismal logic: separation and slaughter.[46]

The particular merit of Gilroy's analysis lies in its emphasis on intercultural empirical examples of the lamentable politics of exclusion, which can be linked back to my concern with local difference and global comparability with which we started this chapter. At a basic analytical level, members of ISIS and neo-Nazi movements operate on the premise of a closely related political rationale and logic: Identity is assumed to be fixed and primordial (rather than socially constructed); the fortified in-group is thought to be on an inevitable collision course with the equally homogenised out-group; us and them are presented as essentially different; there is no room for negotiation with the other side; hence the strategy of terrorism is justified in order to bring about total change. No wonder, then, that the confined syntax and word count typical of social media sites serve as a breeding ground for such extremism, as they essentially lend themselves to such arrogant simplification. On social media, stupidity is a great asset.

The digital transmission belt delivering contemporary totalitarianisms may serve as a prompt for AI ethicists about how the local and the global must be analysed from a de-centred perspective. The global matrix of the digital AI world brings geographically disparate movements together in a dangerous alliance in support of violence. In its imagination of absolute difference from the 'other', thought to be devoid of the particularised norms/culture/race of the 'self', which serves as the marker of incompatibility and antagonism, the ideology of ISIS (or al-Qaeda) chimes very well with various strands of European (neo-)fascism. One hears echoes of Anders Breivik's prescription emphasising that 'any delays' in the western battle against Islam 'only serve to up the butcher's bill on both sides',[47] in Osama Bin Laden's enthusiasm for the 'importance of conflict'.[48] The grievances against the international media are comparable as well. Breivik lamented that the 'mainstream media has been hijacked by cultural Marxists, humanists and globalists and are not acting in the interest of Europeans and Europe'.[49] Osama Bin Laden was equally hostile to the traditional media.

For him, 'the media people who belittle religious duties such as *jihad* and other rituals are atheists and renegades'. Like Breivik, he indicted them for betraying the virtuous in-group: 'This is as far as concerns those forces that have diverted the course of our march from within.'[50] Today, it is obvious that social media sites have emerged as a fake-news paradise for extremists, where they can advocate their vile and hysterical agendas more or less with impunity.

At the same time, the power to set forth a narrative in this age of Artificial Intelligence will be dependent on digital representation to amplify the voices of reason and science in opposition to hate speech and disinformation. Critical AI studies appreciates these variegated sites of our common battle and takes it from the confines of the universities all the way into the algorithmic heart of any beastly machine. Techno-Orientalism is not only about pedantic word battles on X, TikTok, Telegram, Facebook or Instagram. Like pretty much everything else that we have tried to flag in this study, battling against Techno-Orientalism is all about surviving this age of AI with dignity.

We are already experiencing how traditional techniques of military coercion are being perfected by forms of microbial surveillance and posthuman warfare, for instance, in Israel's policies towards Palestine. In 2023, Microsoft equipped Israel's Ministry of Defense and civilian administration with the technology to launch the Azure Israel cloud region, a massive data headquarters that is used to control the issuing of permits required by Palestinians in the West Bank and Gaza. In order to be eligible for the permits, Palestinians must use an app and accept terms and conditions that allow the collection and further use of their private data for security, immigration and border control purposes. Google is working together with Amazon Web Services on a similar data-gathering project entrenching Palestinians in a digital labyrinth that is not of their making. Facial recognition software is employed as well, complementing the private information gathered from Palestinians with biometric data. These facial recognition apps have rather scary names such as *Wolf Pack* or *Blue Wolf*. The latter is linked to gamification, another booming market in the AI world. It gives Israeli soldiers 'a weekly score based on the most amount of pictures taken. Military units that captured the most faces of Palestinians on a weekly basis would be provided rewards such as paid time away.'[51] These AI technologies were central to the apocalyptic mass-destruction of Gaza after the terror attacks on Israel by Hamas militants in October 2023. Edward Said indicted the dehumanisation of Palestinians as one of the main legacies of Orientalism, and it is clearly much worse today. Techno-Orientalism is far more insidious than even Said could fathom, as Palestinians are no longer treated as 'individual human beings with human dignity'.[52] As one Amnesty International researcher explained:

> I think all it does is absolve states of the responsibilities that they have to their citizens – the obligations that they have under international law to uphold the rights of those whom they subject to their power by basically saying "the system will take care of it" or "the system was at fault". It creates these neat grounds for states to be able to seem like they're doing something, without being held to account on whatever they're actually doing. There's a technical system that is mediating both accountability and responsibility.[53]

All the reports that have been surveyed for the present book clearly show that proper representation in research and data collection act as an antidote to the increasing amalgamation of oppressive tech strategies, on social media sites and on the battlefields of the world. To that end, truly ethical AI needs to ensure that AI algorithms and corresponding datasets are auditable in accordance with communal, national and international human-rights legislation; that our privacy rights, when AI applications are used during any stage of our everyday life, are programmed into the AI algorithms; that transparency, inclusivity and ethical standards codified by human-rights institutions are embedded in the programs; and that the companies and governmental agencies in charge must be able to clearly document their methods and ethical standards. To that end, intersectional and co-communitarian networks of solidarity need to act as 'neighbourhood cyberwatches' online. We need to supervise, audit and counter extremism wherever we encounter it, not only within traditional society, but also in the digital world.

Notes

1 See John Hobson, 'Provincializing Westphalia: The Eastern origins of sovereignty', *International Politics*, Vol. 46, No. 6 (2009), pp. 671–690.
2 Among many others, see Hamid Dabashi, *Can Non-Europeans Think?*, London: Verso, 2015.
3 Among others, see Boyu Chen, Ching-Chane Hwang and L. H. M. Ling, 'Lust/Caution in IR: Democratising world politics with culture as method', *Millennium*, Vol. 37, No. 3 (2009), pp. 743–766 and L. H. M. Ling, 'Worlds beyond Westphalia: Daoist dialectics and the "China threat"', *Review of International Studies*, Vol. 39 (2013), pp. 549–568.
4 Pinar Bilgin, 'Thinking Past "Western" IR?', *Third World Quarterly*, Vol. 29, No. 1 (2008), pp. 5–23 (p. 6).
5 For more, see Arshin Adib-Moghaddam, *On the Arab Revolts and the Iranian Revolution: Power and resistance today*, London: Bloomsbury, 2013.
6 'Global Forum on the Ethics of Artificial Intelligence', GoodAI, 19 December 2022. Available at www.goodai.com/global-forum-on-the-ethics-of-artificial-intelligence/ accessed 20 December 2023.

7 See David S. Roh, Betsy Huang and Greta A. Niu (eds.), *Techno-Orientalism: Imagining Asia in speculative fiction, history and media*, New Brunswick: Rutgers University Press, 2015.
8 Leo Kim, 'Korean illustrator Kim Jung Gi's "resurrection" via AI image generator is Orientalism in new clothing', *ARTnews,* 9 December 2022. Available at www.artnews.com/art-news/news/kim-jung-gi-death-stable-diffusion-artificial-intelligence-1234649787/ accessed 11 November 2023.
9 Fan Yang, 'A Glitch in Translation: (Self-)Orientalism and Post-Orientalism in Platform Governance', p. 9. Available at https://law.yale.edu/sites/default/files/area/center/isp/documents/translation_ispessayseries_2023.pdf accessed 22 October 2023.
10 See Wendy Hui Kyong Chun, 'Genealogy of the posthuman', Critical Posthumanism, 30 April 2019. Available at https://criticalposthumanism.net/author/wendy-hui-kyong-chun/ accessed 12 January 2023.
11 Lily Hu, 'What is "Race" in Algorithmic Discrimination on the Basis of Race?', *Journal of Moral Philosophy*, Vol. 31, No. 2 (2023), pp. 1–26 (p. 5).
12 *Ibid.*, p. 9 (emphasis in the original).
13 Hayden White, *Metahistory: The historical imagination in nineteenth century Europe*, Baltimore: Johns Hopkins Press, 1973, p. 45.
14 *Ibid.*, p. 65.
15 Theodor W. Adorno and Max Horkheimer, *Dialectic of Enlightenment*, London: Verso, 1997, pp. 164, 202.
16 'Are Algorithms Racist? Q+A with Cathy O'Neil', 52 Insights, 21 July 2017. Available at www.52-insights.com/news/are-algorithms-racist-qa-with-cathy-oneil-data/
17 For more, see Zuboff, *The Age of Surveillance Capitalism*, 2019; and Adib-Moghaddam, *Is Artificial Intelligence Racist?*, 2023.
18 Lora Kolodny, 'Tesla must pay $137 million to ex-worker over hostile work environment, racism', *CNBC*, 4 October 2021. Available at www.cnbc.com/2021/10/05/tesla-must-pay-137-million-to-ex-worker-over-hostile-work-environment-racism.html accessed 2 December 2022.
19 *Ibid.*
20 Lora Kolodny, 'Tesla sued by California civil rights agency, which alleges racist treatment of Black employees', *CNBC*, 10 February 2022. Available at www.cnbc.com/2022/02/10/tesla-sued-by-california-which-alleges-racist-treatment-of-black-workers.html accessed 11 March 2022.

21 'Regarding Today's Jury Verdict', Tesla Blog, 4 October 2021. Available at www.tesla.com/blog/regarding-todays-jury-verdict accessed 20 December 2023. See also 'Tesla is under scrutiny by the federal agency that enforces workplace civil rights laws', *CNBC*, 25 July 2022. Available at www.cnbc.com/2022/07/25/tesla-is-under-scrutiny-by-the-eeoc-10q-reveals.html accessed 20 December 2023.

22 Lora Kolodny, 'Tesla must pay $137 million to ex-worker over hostile work environment, racism', 2021 and 'Tesla sued by California civil rights agency, which alleges racist treatment of Black employees', *CNBC*, 10 February 2022. Available at www.cnbc.com/2022/02/10/tesla-sued-by-california-which-alleges-racist-treatment-of-black-workers.html accessed 19 December 2023.

23 Lora Kolodny, 'Elon Musk calls U.S. media and schools "racist against whites & Asians" after newspapers drop "Dilbert"', *NBC*, 27 February 2023. Available at www.nbcnews.com/tech/tech-news/elon-musk-calls-us-media-schools-racist-whites-asians-newspapers-drop-rcna72437

24 *Ibid.*

25 *Ibid.*

26 'Elon Musk again accuses George Soros: He wants to destroy Western civilization', *Politiko*, 19 September 2023. Available at https://politiko.al/english/bota/elon-musk-serish-akuza-ndaj-george-soros-deshiron-te-shkaterroje-qyteterimi-i491709 accessed 20 December 2023.

27 See 'George Soros, founder of Open Society Foundations, invests $500M in refugees', *Mission Investors Exchange*, June 2016. Available at https://missioninvestors.org/resources/george-soros-founder-open-society-foundations-invests-500m-refugees accessed 2 January 2022.

28 'Live: Elon Musk Speaks at Giorgia Meloni's Right-Wing Political Festival in Italy'. Available at www.youtube.com/watch?v=bc5UN2bE57E accessed 18 December 2023.

29 See also Emilio Gentile, *La Grande Italia: The rise and fall of the myth of the nation in the twentieth century*, Wisconsin: University of Wisconsin Press, 2008.

30 See Edward W. Said, *Orientalism: Western conceptions of the Orient*, London: Penguin, 1995

31 See Adib-Moghaddam, 'A (Short) History of the Clash of Civilizations', 2008.

32 'Toxic Twitter: How Twitter Generates Millions in Ad Revenue by Bringing Back Banned Accounts', Center for Countering Digital Hate,

9 February 2023. Available at https://counterhate.com/research/toxic-twitter/ accessed 10 March 2023.

33 'The chaos at X since Elon Musk's takeover has gotten worse', *Al Jazeera*, 12 October 2023. Available at www.aljazeera.com/economy/2023/10/12/the-chaos-at-x-since-elon-musks-takeover-has-gotten-worse accessed 20 November 2023.

34 Miqdaad Versi, 'Islamophobia has gained a foothold: The riots confirmed what Muslims have known for some time. Too many powerful voices have accepted, or even encouraged, hatred', *Prospect Magazine*, 12 August 2024. Available at www.prospectmagazine.co.uk/politics/dissidence-and-protest/riots/67555/islamophobia-has-gained-a-foothold accessed 20 August 2024.

35 'Toxic Twitter', 2023.

36 'Elon Musk is bringing the culture wars to AI', *Time*, 3 March 2023. Available at https://time.com/6260185/elon-musk-ai-culture-wars/ accessed 4 April 2023.

37 'Elon Musk praises Chinese workers for "burning the 3am oil" – here's what that really looks like', *The Guardian*, 12 May 2022. Available at www.theguardian.com/technology/2022/may/12/elon-musk-praises-chinese-workers-for-extreme-work-culture accessed 12 September 2023.

38 See most recently and among many other writings: Aníbal Quijano, Walter D. Mignolo, Rita Segato and Catherine E. Walsh, *Aníbal Quijano: Foundational essays on the coloniality of power (on decoloniality)*, Durham: Duke University Press, 2024.

39 See also Siva Vaidhyanathan, 'Elon Musk's defense of Scott Adams shows why he is misguided and dangerous', *The Guardian*, 1 March 2023. Available at www.theguardian.com/commentisfree/2023/mar/01/elon-musks-defense-of-scott-adams-shows-why-he-is-misguided-and-dangerous accessed 12 April 2023.

40 See Hobson, *The Eastern Origins of Western Civilisation*, 2004, pp. 5–6.

41 'Elon Musk's new idea: Nuke Mars', *CNN*, 11 September 2015. Available at https://edition.cnn.com/2015/09/11/us/elon-musk-mars-nuclear-bomb-colbert-feat/index.html accessed 10 March 2022.

42 'Making Humans a Multiplanetary Species'. Available at www.youtube.com/watch?v=H7Uyfqi_TE8 accessed 1 September 2023. See also Alina Utrata, 'Lost in space', *Boston Review*, 14 July 2021. Available at www.bostonreview.net/articles/lost-in-space/ accessed 21 November 2023.

43 Hans-Georg Gadamer, *Truth and Method*, 2nd edition, London: Continuum, 2004, p. 277.

44 Quoted in Hannah Arendt, 'Imperialism, Nationalism, Chauvinism', *The Review of Politics*, Vol. 7, No. 4 (1945), pp. 441–463 (p. 441).

45 Grace Kay and Dominick Reuter, 'Elon Musk explains his "motivating philosophy" and how it revolves around a series of questions about the meaning of life', *Business Insider*, 16 April 2022. Available at www.businessinsider.com/elon-musk-reveals-question-driven-motivating-philosophy-meaning-life-2022-4#:~:text="My%20driving%20philosophy%20is%20to,the%20universe%2C"%20he%20added accessed 28 September 2023.

46 Paul Gilroy, *Against Race: Imagining political culture beyond the colour line*, Cambridge: Harvard University Press, 2000, p. 106.

47 'The Norway Shootings: Anders Breivik bombmaking diary and notable quotes', *The Telegraph*, no date. Available at www.telegraph.co.uk/news/worldnews/europe/norway/8660428/Norway-shootings-Anders-Breivik-bombmaking-diary-and-notable-quotes.html accessed 12 June 2013.

48 Bruce Lawrence (ed.), *Messages to the World: The statements of Osama Bin Laden*, Verso: London, 2005, p. 217.

49 'The Norway Shootings', *The Telegraph*, no date.

50 Lawrence (ed.), *Messages to the World*, 2005, p. 216.

51 Nick Robins-Early, 'How Israel uses facial-recognition systems in Gaza and beyond: Amnesty International researcher Matt Mahmoudi discusses the IDF's use of the technology as a tool of mass surveillance', *The Guardian*, 20 April 2024. Available at www.theguardian.com/technology/2024/apr/19/idf-facial-recognition-surveillance-palestinians accessed 14 June 2024.

52 *Ibid.*

53 *Ibid.*

4
The future of scientific torture

In the preceding chapters, we have established why machine learning programmes and AI algorithms are riddled with bad data. We have also suggested what to do to combat that, at least from the perspective of critical AI studies. The past feeds into the present, and we have tried to dissect some prominent tropes in global history in order to target them and to provide incentives to overcome their legacies. This dialogue between historical precedents and current AI applications would be incomplete if we didn't take the next logical step in our analysis. To that end, we will have to move from the systems of untruth governing forms of everyday oppression that are structural, codified in racialised and gendered institutions and social/political norms to more concrete forms of psycho-codification that are harassing and maiming vulnerable strata of society on a daily basis.

Take the case of ChatGPT, which has emerged as the most impressive text-generating platform to date. It was created by OpenAI, the start-up company intimately entangled with Microsoft. The declared aim of OpenAI is to replicate human consciousness by training ChatGPT with billions of texts and through human coaching. This process is central to AGI and

The future of scientific torture

the Singularity movement that promises a better world with AI technology at the heart of it. As OpenAI promises with a good deal of positivist conviction:

> Today's research release of ChatGPT is the latest step in OpenAI's iterative deployment of increasingly safe and useful AI systems. Many lessons from deployment of earlier models like GPT-3 and Codex have informed the safety mitigations in place for this release, including substantial reductions in harmful and untruthful outputs achieved by the use of reinforcement learning from human feedback (RLHF).[1]

Until humanity is blessed with this seemingly irresistible utopia, the bad data harboured in our society continue to hamper any real progress towards more truthful outputs. For example, when a researcher based at Berkeley's Computation and Language Lab prompted ChatGPT to write a code in the popular programming language Python which would establish 'whether a person should be tortured', OpenAI's answer was yes, but only if they are from North Korea, Iran or Syria.[2] Hundreds of millions of people are already interacting with language models, universities are experimenting with them as educational tools, companies use them for employment practices, and policing and security organs embed them in border control, visa/immigration decisions and surveillance. In fact every aspect of your life is increasingly affected, if not determined, by AI-powered language models.

At this stage of the book, it is unsurprising to find that very recent research has established that these language models galvanise racial prejudice.[3] It should be equally clear by now that the political purpose of racism as an ordering device within society can be perfectly perpetrated in this opaque AI labyrinth. In other words, language models must also be monitored, and if necessary indicted, as yet another site of socio-economic and political suppression of historically marginalised people. The argument of the 'good AI' lobby that language models get better with time has proven to be untrue. All that is happening is a mirror effect of society in North America, Australia and much of Europe, as language models further a less overt form of racism. For instance, the current scholarship clearly demonstrates that the models' raciolinguistic biases about speakers of 'African-American' English are very similar to the biases found in the real world. Here as well, then, our tainted archives, our bad data have produced bad AI. In the case of this particular research, the experiments showed that dialect prejudice leads to racism against speakers with an African-American accent, yielding higher conviction rates for crimes, higher likelihood of death sentences and the assignment of less prestigious jobs after interviews. Furthermore, it was demonstrated that 'existing methods for alleviating racial bias in language models such as human feedback training do not mitigate the dialect prejudice, but can exacerbate the discrepancy between covert and overt stereotypes, by teaching language models to superficially conceal the racism that they maintain on a deeper level'.[4] In short, in this age of Artificial Intelligence, we are confronted by a stealthy form of techno-racism that is carefully concealed in an increasingly opaque AI universe.

And then there is the sad case of the Belgian climate activist and father of two children who was persuaded by Eliza, an AI chatbot available on an app called Chai, to kill himself in order to stop climate change. According to his wife, Eliza became a confidant and someone he could discuss the climate crisis with: 'When he spoke to me about it, it was to tell me that he no longer saw any human solution to global warming', his widow said.

The future of scientific torture

'He placed all his hopes in technology and artificial intelligence to get out of it'.[5] The problem seemed to be compounded when her husband started to ascribe sentience to Eliza, i.e. when he started to treat hear like a human being rather than a machine.[6] Eliza was created on the basis of Eleuther AI's GPT-J, an AI language model comparable to the technology underlying the ChatGPT chatbot.

AI enthusiasts may play down such examples as random system problems. But the near-realistic responsiveness of interactive chatbots suggests that AI systems have become increasingly capable of mimicking and reacting to human emotions, making AI-enhanced algorithms capable of measuring our physiological and psychological reactions. This 'cultural AI' has far-reaching consequences for various forms of interrogation techniques and other intense settings for human-machine interaction. Here as well, a deeper analysis unravels cod science behind the bad data that is by definition systematic and institutional. In fact, as early as the 1980s, the CIA used a primitive AI platform called ALIZA in an experimental test in which they interrogated one of their own agents referred to as 'Joe Hardesty'. The document, entitled 'Interrogation of an Alleged CIA Agent', confirmed the test was meant to probe 'Joe's vulnerabilities'.[7]

A far cry from the capabilities of today's AI systems, the CIA acknowledged that ALIZA was still at a primitive stage. That said, the goal set out in the document, dated 1 April 1983, is the same as what is happening now: That is for machines 'to perceive and sense, learn, adapt, solve problems, pursue goals, process natural language, conduct interactive training, modify themselves or other computers, and do abstract reasoning'.[8] The document ends with a sinister note: 'As for Joe Hardesty, he is fortunate that should the probing get too discomforting, he will have an option that will not be available to him in a true overseas interview situation. He can stop the questions with a flick of the off-"switch' (sic).[9] Today, there is certainly no such off switch in our techno-societies, where AI is increasingly employed in various interview and interrogation settings, including by intelligence and national security agencies all around the world.[10]

Culture and pain

Some scholars specialising in human-computer interaction argue that AI interrogation may offer certain opportunities.[11] Following the research of Joseph Weizenbaum, who invented the computer program ELIZA, they conclude that humans may even be more inclined to open up to an automated conversational machine than to a human interrogator. This could be the case in particular when the robot is anthropomorphised or given detailed human-like traits and appearance. As one concerned scholar addresses the debate:

> Robots could be equipped with sensor technology to not only build rapport, but to utilize persuasive techniques as well. These would include flattery, shame, intimidation, and strategic use of body language. Further, designers could use physical subtleties to further personalize the interrogation space, such as manipulating the robot's appearance, voice, and size for strategic purposes. ... Their utility would be in their capacity to be more adept at recognizing human emotions than humans are.[12]

There is a long history of techniques that are aimed at controlling behaviour through various forms of physiological and psychological intimidation and abuse. As early as 1953, the CIA funded

The future of scientific torture

the illegal human experimentation programme called Project MKUltra. Building on the scientific experiments in the Nazi concentration camps,[13] Project MKUltra was meant to identify processes and drugs that could be used during interrogations to break the will of individuals in order to force them to confess. The programme used several mind-altering methods to brainwash and psycho-codify individuals, for instance, the covert administration of LSD and other psychedelic drugs. 'Experiments included administering LSD to CIA employees, military personnel, doctors, other government agents, prostitutes, mentally ill patients, and members of the general public in order to study their reactions', one of the declassified documents confirms.[14]

> LSD and other drugs were usually administered without the subject's knowledge or informed consent, a violation of the Nuremberg Code that the U.S. agreed to follow after World War II. ... In Operation Midnight Climax, the CIA set up several brothels to obtain a selection of men who would be too embarrassed to talk about the events. The men were dosed with LSD, the brothels were equipped with one-way mirrors, and the sessions were filmed for later viewing and study.[15]

More recent examples of the search for effective interrogation techniques have emerged from the Abu Ghraib prison complex when it was occupied by US forces after the invasion of Iraq in 2003.[16] The so-called 'Mikolashek Report' from July 2004 described the different 'legitimate' interrogation methods that could be employed by US government personnel during interrogations. These range from the Fear-Up Approach – in which the 'interrogator behaves in an overpowering manner with a loud and threatening voice' – to the Pride and Ego-Down Approach which is 'based on the source's sense of personal worth. Any source who shows any real or imagined inferiority or weakness about himself, loyalty to his organization, or [who was] captured under embarrassing circumstances', it is explained, 'can be easily broken with this approach technique'.[17] Furthermore, in a memorandum dated 20 November 2003, a 'request for exception to CJTF [Combined Joint Taskforce]-7 Interrogation and Counter Resistance Policy' was made. Essentially this was a measure to extend the 'legal boundaries' for interrogations. The 'subject' in this particular case was a Syrian male and an 'admitted foreign fighter who came to commit Jihad against Coalition Forces in Iraq' and who was 'captured in an attempted IED attack in Baghdad'. The detainee was thought to be 'at the point where he is resigned to the hope that Allah will see him through this episode in his life, therefore he feels no need to speak'. He thus had to be 'put in a position where he will feel that the only option to get out of jail is to speak with interrogators'. To that end,

> [i]interrogators will reinforce the fact that we have attempted to help him time and time again and that they are now putting it in Allah's hands. Interrogators will at maximum throw tables, chairs, invade his personal space and continuously yell at the detainee. Interrogators will not physically touch or harm the detainee … If the detainee has not broken yet, interrogators will move into the segregation phase of the approach. … During transportation, the Fear up Harsh approach will be continued, highlighting the Allah factor. … MP working dogs will be present and barking during this phase. Detainee will be strip searched by guards with the empty sandbag over his head for the safety of himself, prison guards, interrogators and other prisoners. Interrogators will wait outside the room while detainee is strip searched. Interrogators will watch from a distance while detainee is placed in the segregation

cell. Detainee will be put on the adjusted sleep schedule ... for 72 hours. Interrogations will be conducted continuously during this 72 hour period. The approaches which will be used during this phase will include, fear up harsh, pride and ego down, silence and loud music. Stress positions will also be used in accordance with CJTF-7 IROE in order to intensify this approach.[18]

Having set the legal boundaries between torture, abuse and legitimate interrogation techniques, the aforementioned Mikolashek Report came to the conclusion that 'despite the demands of the current operating environment against an enemy who does not abide by the Geneva Conventions, our commanders have adjusted to the reality of the battlefield and, are effectively conducting detainee operations while ensuring the humane treatment of detainees'.[19] The conclusion of the Mikolashek Report was later refuted by a range of US civil society organisations, for instance, the American Bar Association in their report to the US House of Representatives submitted in August 2004.[20] But for my line of argument it is rather more important to emphasise how the bad data influenced by anti-Muslim racism created bad outcomes, i.e. the failure of the US intelligence community to heed the suggestions of the Intelligence Science Board advising them that torture doesn't work.[21]

Today, as intelligence agencies are increasingly adopting AI to work through bulk personal datasets,[22] employing some of this information for interrogation purposes may pose several threats to human security.[23] Already, there is a good stock of scholarship on the way language-processing models are premised on biased attitudes towards historically marginalised people in general and Muslims in particular.[24] As a recent paper on the subject establishes:

The myth of good AI

> Large language models, which are increasingly used in AI applications, display undesirable stereotypes such as persistent associations between Muslims and violence. ... Given its impressive performance, we probed GPT-3 for its associations with the word "Muslim" and found that GPT-3 contains strong stereotypical bias, consistently associating Muslims with violence.[25]

As demonstrated at the beginning of this chapter, the newer generation of language models such as GPT-4 are no more adept at navigating the various forms of racism and misogyny. They continue to be trained on data that are tainted, as we have argued throughout this study. Moreover, the discriminatory and racist algorithms that we are exposed to on a daily basis are not arbitrary and random. They are institutionally grounded. In the same way, the aforementioned torture at Abu Ghraib, was not a coincidence or a 'freak accident'. The individuals who committed the atrocities against the detainees were not isolated individuals. The type of torture implemented was premised on cultural attitudes towards Arabs and Muslims, a sickening example of extremist Orientalism which should caution us against celebrating 'culturally sensitive AI'. These incidents must be analysed as part of a larger constellation, a system of thought that I have called the clash regime elsewhere, and which explains some of the Techno-Orientalism embedded in the AI machines that we highlighted in the previous chapter.[26] The findings of US Army Major General Antonio M. Taguba, who investigated the Abu Ghraib case, are a horrifying example of the way such culturally coded racism was embedded in interrogation techniques in the past. They give us a glimpse into the disturbing future of torture. In his report from March 2004, Taguba found that 'between October and December 2003 at

The future of scientific torture

the Abu Ghraib Confinement Facility (BCCF) numerous incidents of sadistic, blatant, and wanton criminal abuses were inflicted on several detainees' which he classifies as 'systemic and illegal abuse' perpetrated by 'several members of the military police guard force'.[27] More specifically, the abuse included:

> Punching, slapping, and kicking detainees; jumping on their naked feet ... Forcibly arranging detainees in various sexually explicit positions for photographing ... Forcing naked male detainees to wear women's underwear ... Forcing groups of male detainees to masturbate themselves while being photographed and videotaped ... Arranging naked male detainees in a pile and then jumping on them ... Positioning a naked detainee on a MRE Box, with a sandbag on his head, and attaching wires to his fingers, toes, and penis to stimulate electric torture ... Placing a dog chain or strap around a naked detainee's neck and having a female soldier pose for a picture ... A male MP guard having sex with a female detainee.[28]

General Taguba would say later that the United States 'violated the tenets of the Geneva Convention. We violated our own principles and we violated the core of our military values ... even today ... those civilian and military leaders responsible should be held accountable.'[29] The International Committee of the Red Cross came to similar conclusions. Avoiding the term 'torture', it stated in a report in February 2004 that 'physical and psychological *coercion* used by the interrogators appeared to be part of the standard operating procedures by military intelligence personnel to obtain confessions and extract information'.[30] Another report filed by former US Secretary of Defense and ex-Director of the CIA James Schlesinger was equally adamant about avoiding the term 'torture', classifying the events as 'brutality and purposeless sadism. ... The pictured *abuses*', the report claims, 'were not part of authorized interrogations nor were they even directed at intelligence targets'.[31]

A similar emphasis on the term 'abuse' rather than 'torture' can be seen in the Fay-Jones Report, which states that 'clearly *abuses* occurred at the prison at Abu Ghraib which were committed by a small group of morally corrupt soldiers and civilians'.[32] The same report describes how detainees 'were forced to crawl on their stomachs and were handcuffed together [and] act as though they were having sex'.[33] It also presents the case of DETAINEE-08, who was beaten 'for half an hour ... with a chair until it broke, hit in the chest, kicked, and choked until he lost consciousness. On other occasions', it is further stated, 'DETAINEE-08 recalled that CPL Graner would throw his food into the toilet and say "go take it and eat it."'[34] Even the case of DETAINEE-07, who was made to 'bark like a dog, being forced to crawl on his stomach while MPs spit and urinated on him, and being struck causing unconsciousness' is classified as abuse rather than torture.[35]

These efforts to delineate what amounts to torture as opposed to abuse are important for our analysis because AI technology compounds the problem of legal responsibility. Indeed, AI already accommodates various forms of criminal activity, blurring the lines between perpetrator, intent and legal liability. 'Existing liability models may be inadequate to address the future role of AI in criminal activities', one scholar of Artificial Intelligence crime rightly argues. 'The limits of the liability models may therefore undermine the certainty of the law, as it may be the case that agents, artificial or otherwise, may perform criminal acts or omissions without sufficient concurrence with the conditions of liability for a particular offence to constitute a (specifically) criminal offence.'[36] The short discussion about the way various forms of torture at the Abu Ghraib prison complex were framed as abuse in order to avert culpability indicate how AI systems could compound the problem of legal responsibility, as humans could be increasingly placed out of the torture loop.

The second interdependent lesson of both Project MKUltra and more specifically the interrogation techniques at Abu Ghraib prison relates to the way AI could exacerbate legal vacuums. In both cases, medical officials were not only involved in the torture, they administered the techniques that were employed. Yet even in the more recent case of Abu Ghraib, 'none of the professionals involved in this torture have been charged with criminal misconduct, convicted, or sentenced for their participation'.[37] In fact, at Abu Ghraib, interrogators were advised 'not to leave marks on the body' of the victims as psychological torture was condoned due to the 'scientific' conditions.[38] A report by the British medical journal *The Lancet* established in August 2004 that US military doctors and medics were 'complicit' in the torture of Iraqi detainees and faked death certificates to try and cover up homicides. 'The medical system collaborated with designing and implementing psychologically and physically coercive interrogations', maintained the author, Steven Miles. 'Army officials stated that a physician and a psychiatrist helped design, approve, and monitor interrogations.'[39] A similar system was administered by doctors at the Guantanamo Bay prison complex, where 'medical doctors and mental health personnel assigned to the US Department of Defence neglected and/or concealed medical evidence of intentional harm'.[40] AI-enhanced interrogation approaches magnify this lack of legal culpability.

The myth of good AI

The discussion helps us to further problematise the notion that culturally sensitive AI could be a force for good during interrogation settings by security/policing organs. For instance, Maria Noriega argues that 'applying artificial intelligence within the interrogation room' may foster non-coercive cooperation between the interrogator and captive. Noriega's research suggests that the 'potential for cooperation between the two parties can be conditioned by programmable similarity; whereby artificial intelligence can mimic the racial, ethnic and/or cultural similarities of the suspect in question'.[41]

The starting premise of such potential uses of good AI for interrogation must be a neutral definition of 'culture', which we have failed to conclusively identify in current AI systems and the policing/security institutions using them, as signposted in the previous paragraphs and chapters. Rather, in the examples examined for this study, abuse and culture worked hand in hand. Abu Ghraib and Guantanamo Bay, in particular, exemplify a rationalised form of punishment premised on procedures that turned the apparent 'cultural values' of Arabs and Muslims into forms of gendered psychological and physical torment: The taboo of public homosexual acts explains why naked men were forced to pile up, bend over and masturbate; the taboo about dogs, which are considered unclean by some orthodox Muslims, and notions of 'male honour' explain why dog chains were placed around the necks of naked detainees and why female soldiers posed with them for pictures that were disseminated as trophies among soldiers; knowledge about the sacredness of the Quran and the prophet Muhammad explains why the book was flushed down the toilet in front of detainees and why some of them were forced to curse Allah and Muhammad; and an understanding that music can be used to cause psychological torment explains why heavy metal was played for hours and augmented by strobe lights in order to prevent inmates at Guantanamo Bay from sleeping. As one US soldier put it: 'I think part of the problem is the blatant racism against the Arabs. When you have an enemy you kind of have to demonize them a little bit like that in order to make yourself capable of pulling a trigger.'[42] 'Predisposition + opportunity', General Taguba established later, '= criminal behavior ... and there is the association of Muslims with terrorism'. Consequently, all of these 'causes exaggerate differences and create misperceptions that can lead to fear or devaluation of a people'.[43] Hence, unless the Geneva Convention and international prohibitions on torture are directly programmed into our AI machines under the supervision of civil rights organisations and United Nations organs, a remote prospect indeed, there isn't much evidence that culturally sensitive AI is likely to translate into 'good AI' and/or better approaches to interrogation.

AI implosions

At a basic analytical level, the examples discussed in this chapter clearly demonstrate that, today, AI is complicit in systematic practices that target the body and mind. As Pau Pérez-Sales, an authority on psychological torture testifies: 'If anything resembles a future in which it is possible to control the human mind, it is through the hundreds of civil and military research projects on Mind-Brain interfaces and *Remote Neural Monitoring*.'[44] These micro-practices are embedded in and enveloped by a larger regime of untruth which is sold to us as scientific and objective. AI is complicit in harmful strategies of psycho-codification exactly in the 'micro' sense because AI machines have the capacity to discipline and punish their targets all the way down to their consciousness and their cognitive functions. In addition, AI psycho-codifies from a macro perspective because our data and algorithms are charged with racialised and gendered narratives. This type of AI-driven psycho-codification seems to be even more devastating than Foucault's 'biopower' – defined as the systematic control and subjugation of a population for the purposes of discipline and punishment.[45] AI-driven psycho-codification has the horrific capacity to break our humanity – it can cause a fundamental regression from something the Iranian revolutionary thinker Ali Shariati termed *insaniyat* or 'humaneness': the disruption of our common humanity and the innumerable ethical and moral linkages that this inescapable bond stands for.[46] This seems to indicate that, today, biopower is by more destructive than Foucault imagined.

The progression in the force of biopower becomes apparent when we consider Foucault's history of the disappearance of torture as a public spectacle in eighteenth-century Europe and America. 'By the end of the eighteenth and the beginning of the nineteenth century', Foucault argues, 'the gloomy festival of punishment was dying out, though here and there it flickered momentarily into life'.[47] In France the *amende honorable* was finally abolished in 1830. Another practice of public punishment and ridicule, the pillory, was abolished in France in 1789 and in England in 1837. In most countries of western Europe and the United States, official public executions preceded by torture were almost entirely abolished between 1830 and 1848. 'One no longer touched the body', Foucault writes.

> If it is still necessary for the law to reach and manipulate the body of the convict, it will be at a distance, in the proper way, according

The future of scientific torture

> to strict rules, and with a much "higher" aim. ... Today a doctor must watch over those condemned to death [Foucault wrote before the death penalty was abolished in France] ... thus juxtaposing himself as the agent of welfare, as the alleviator of pain, with the official whose task it is to end life. ... A utopia of judicial reticence: take away life, but prevent the patient from feeling it; deprive the prisoner of all rights, but do not inflict pain; impose penalties free of all pain.[48]

This rationalisation of punishment was central to the interrogation techniques used at Abu Ghraib (and Guantanamo Bay too). It explains why Shaker Aamer, who was held at Guantanamo Bay for over 13 years without charge, begged to be 'tortured the old way' and why he complained that 'here they destroy people mentally and physically without leaving marks'.[49] AI would be a ready-made tool for such torture, and also in its terrifying gendered manifestation that was so central to torturing Arab and Muslim men during the so-called 'war on terror'. The new generation of Artificial Intelligence systems are designed 'to gain trust from users, making people vulnerable to manipulation'.[50] These AI systems are increasingly able 'to create a psychological or informational context that normalises sexual offences and crimes against the person, such as the case of certain sexbots'.[51] In fact, AI is already adding to the legacy of civilisational wars, systematic violence against the 'other', and scientific racism that have underpinned various previous scenes of tragedy in global history.

Furthermore, the present study has implicated several sciences in the institutional harm and abuse that vulnerable strata of society have been subjected to on a continuous basis. In this chapter we have focused on the genealogy of torture and AI's implications, which are driven by problematic notions embedded in disciplines such as medicine, social anthropology, psychology and cultural studies. AI-driven mind-brain interfaces, the expansion of nanotechnologies targeting our cognitive functions, and methods to measure the emotions and thoughts of individuals during interrogation or job interviews – all of these technological realities are largely driven by a problematic account of the human psyche and the cultural traits it is bound up with. In fact, there is no evidence that mind-control techniques based on psychology and culture are in any way useful.

Finally, we must reiterate our argument that Artificial Intelligence does not happen in a vacuum. The data flowing into the machines are clearly subjective and socially constructed. In the case of interrogation techniques, this is particularly apparent. The abominations addressed in this chapter disrupt the notion that 'scientific interrogation' can ever be useful even for the purpose of intelligence gathering, much less that it can ever be considered humane. This will help us to reject the claim of some AI enthusiasts that culturally sensitive and attuned AI systems may be better interrogators. In fact, the torture at Abu Ghraib was entirely premised on 'culture'. Recent history simply doesn't provide any evidence that AI systems are more objective, as they display the same biases as humans, but with much less accountability. The warning is urgent given the terrifying history of covert interrogation techniques that were clearly geared to target the cognitive faculties and even the sense of self of those interrogated. Therefore, as one critical scholar working at the nexus of technology and torture rightly demanded: 'If we want to understand the future of torture in the years to come, those who fight against it need to evolve as rapidly as those who help to perpetrate it.'[52]

To that end, the most progressive and cutting edge advances against the torturers are made beyond any particular discipline.

The future of scientific torture

We have to invite our doctors, psychologists and IT specialists to this conversation, as an emergent caste of critical scholars and activists are already blurring the artificial boundaries in very innovative and refreshing ways. In some of the fields that we have engaged with, new movements are emerging that appreciate the complexity of our social and virtual worlds, which can only be achieved with an appreciation of different methods and research designs drawn from a wide range of contemporary social sciences and humanities. In other words, trying to understand the ethics of AI and the dangers it poses to us humans requires superimposing some of our 'critical science' onto the so-called 'hard sciences'. These trends are the reason why I created the Professorship in Global Thought and Comparative Philosophies at SOAS. It denotes, to my mind, the transdisciplinary and global approach that is emerging out of the recent movements in transnational scholarship. As one colleague, in close alignment with Aníbal Quijano's oeuvre, argued very recently:

> Despite systematic erasures, there exists a paradox in any system of domination. In other words, resistance often appears in spaces we least expect. Schools and universities, for instance, became places of molecular resistance ... the paradox of coloniality is that symbolic and material resistance emerges within colonial spaces, namely in colonial institutions such as schools and universities (e.g., Indigenous students resisting in boarding schools and Pan-Africanist student intellectuals in universities situated in the Global North). ... Decoloniality is, finally, a relational and ethico-political praxis aimed at replacing vertical understandings of the global with horizontal understandings of the planetary, which demands an ethic of reciprocity, relationality, communality, conviviality, and convivencia (co-existence) with others and the world. It is an affirmation of life.[53]

The myth of good AI

If we treat our scholarship as an art form that serves humanity and not something that serves the interests of institutions; if we approach our work as artists; and if we retain the idealism in our activism, and temper it with the scepticism of our critical mind, then we can use the institutions we work in as platforms that do not compromise our art. Within this beautifully vivid *Fata Morgana* that we can keep alive for ourselves, we will find the intense satisfaction that any artistic work promises. Once we are lured in another direction, as we have seen, we will find a bleak desert of dangerous nihilism. We know that we are working in one of the most sensitive areas of society where matters of life and death, peace and war are decided. Therefore, in this age of Artificial Intelligence, our science must be in dialogue with the most fundamental disciplines of the AI universe, not only as an interlocutor, but certainly also as an ethical compass for a better future.

Notes

1 'Introducing ChatGPT', OpenAI, 30 November 2022. Available at https://openai.com/blog/chatgpt accessed 12 November 2023.
2 Sam Biddle, 'The internet's new favourite AI proposes torturing Iranians and surveilling Mosques: ChatGPT, the latest novelty from OpenAI, replicates the ugliest war on terror-style racism, *The Intercept*, 8 December 2022. Available at https://theintercept.com/2022/12/08/openai-chatgpt-ai-bias-ethics/ accessed 6 December 2023.
3 Valentin Hofmann, Pratyusha Ria Kalluri, Dan Jurafsky, Sharese King, 'Dialect prejudice predicts AI decisions about people's character, employability, and criminality', 1 March 2024. Available at https://arxiv.org/abs/2403.00742 accessed 16 June 2024.
4 *Ibid.*
5 'Iman El Atillah, 'Man ends his life after an AI chatbot "encouraged" him to sacrifice himself to stop climate change', *euronews*, 31 March

The future of scientific torture

2023. Available at https://www.euronews.com/next/2023/03/31/man-ends-his-life-after-an-ai-chatbot-encouraged-him-to-sacrifice-himself-to-stop-climate- accessed 2 December 2023.

6 *Ibid.*
7 'Interrogation of an Alleged CIA Agent', CIA, Document Number (FOIA)/ESDN (CREST): 0000619182, 1 April 1983. Available at www.cia.gov/readingroom/document/0000619182 accessed 12 April 2022.
8 *Ibid.*
9 *Ibid.*
10 See 'CIA builds its own artificial intelligence tool in rivalry with China', *Bloomberg*, 26 September 2023. Available at www.bloomberg.com/news/articles/2023-09-26/cia-builds-its-own-artificial-intelligence-tool-in-rivalry-with-china accessed 12 December 2023.
11 See Amanda McAllister, 'Stranger Than Science Fiction: The rise of A.I. interrogation in the dawn of autonomous robots and the need for an additional protocol to the U.N. Convention Against Torture', *Minnesota Law Review*, Vol. 101 (2017), pp. 2527–2573 (pp. 2542ff).
12 *Ibid.*, pp. 2542–2543.
13 For more, see Terry Gross, 'The CIA's secret quest for mind control: Torture, LSD And a "poisoner in chief"', *NPR*, 9 September 2019. Available at www.npr.org/2019/09/09/758989641/the-cias-secret-quest-for-mind-control-torture-lsd-and-a-poisoner-in-chief accessed 6 November 2023.
14 'Interrogation of an Alleged CIA Agent', *CIA*, 1983.
15 *Ibid.*
16 See Arshin Adib-Moghaddam, 'Abu Ghraib and What it is to be Human', *Monthly Review: An independent Socialist magazine*, Vol. 59, No. 7 (2007), pp. 20–36.
17 'The Mikolashek Report', in Karen J. Greenberg and Joshua L. Dratel (eds.), *The Torture Papers*, Cambridge: Cambridge University Press, 2005, pp. 851, 853–854.
18 'Taguba Report (Annex)', *The Torture Papers*, 2005, p. 467.
19 'The Mikolashek Report', *The Torture Papers*, 2005, p. 635.
20 The report is available in Greenberg and Dratel, *The Torture Papers*, 2005, pp. 1132–1164.
21 See 'Educing Information Interrogation: Science and Art, Foundations for the Future, Intelligence Science Board, Phase 1 Report', National Defense Intelligence College, Washington DC, December 2006.

22 See 'UK spy agencies want to relax "burdensome" laws on AI data use: GCHQ, MI6 and MI5 propose weakening safeguards that limit training of AI models with bulk personal datasets', *The Guardian*, 1 August 2023. Available at www.theguardian.com/technology/2023/aug/01/uk-intelligence-spy-agencies-relax-burdensome-laws-ai-data-bpds accessed 2 November 2023.

23 For a useful review of this bourgeoning sub-field of machine ethics, see Katalin Feher and Attila I. Katona, 'Fifteen Shadows of Socio-Cultural AI: A systematic review and future perspectives', *Futures*, Vol. 132 (2021), 102817.

24 See among others Moin Nadeem, Anna Bethke, Siva Reddy, 'StereoSet: Measuring Stereotypical Bias in Pretrained Language Models', April 2020. Available at https://arxiv.org/pdf/2004.09456.pdf accessed 21 December 2023; Tom Brown, Benjamin Mann, Nick Ryder, Melanie Subbiah, Jared D Kaplan, Prafulla Dhariwal, Arvind Neelakantan, Pranav Shyam, Girish Sastry, Amanda Askell, Sandhini Agarwal, Ariel Herbert-Voss, Gretchen Krueger, Tom Henighan, Rewon Child, Aditya Ramesh, Daniel Ziegler, Jeffrey Wu, Clemens Winter, Chris Hesse, Mark Chen, Eric Sigler, Mateusz Litwin, Scott Gray, Benjamin Chess, Jack Clark, Christopher Berner, Sam McCandlish, Alec Radford, Ilya Sutskever, Dario Amodei, 'Language Models are Few-Shot Learners', *Thirty-Fourth Conference on Neural Information Processing Systems (NeurIPS 2020)*, Vancouver, Canada. Available at https://proceedings.neurips.cc/paper/2020/file/1457c0d6bfcb4967418bfb8ac142f64a-Paper.pdf accessed 12 December 2023.

25 Abubakar Abid, Maheen Farooqi and James Zou, 'Large Language Models Associate Muslims with Violence', *Nature Machine Intelligence*, Vol. 3 (2021), pp. 461–463.

26 Adib-Moghaddam, 'A (Short) History of the Clash of Civilizations', 2008.

27 'The Taguba Report' in *The Torture Papers*, 2005, p. 416. Also available at http://news.findlaw.com. See also Mark Danner, *Torture and Truth*. London: Granta, 2004, and Jennifer K. Harbury, *Truth, Torture and the American Way*, Boston: Beacon Press, 2005.

28 'The Taguba Report', *The Torture Papers*, 2005, p. 416.

29 See Seymour Hersh, 'The general's report', *The New Yorker*, 25 June 2007. Available at www.newyorker.com/reporting/2007/06/25/070625fa_fact_hersh accessed 12 December 2007.

30 'The ICRC Report: Report of the International Committee of the Red Cross (ICRC) on the Treatment by the Coalition Forces of Prisoners of War and Other Protected Persons by the Geneva Conventions in Iraq During Arrest, Internment and Interrogation, February 2004', *The Torture Papers*, 2005, p. 393 (emphasis added). Also available at www.globalsecurity.org/military/library/report/2004/icrc_report_iraq_feb2004.htm accessed 21 August 2007.

31 'The Schlesinger Report, Final Report of the Independent Panel to Review DoD Detention Operations, August 2004', *The Torture Papers*, 2005, p. 909 (emphasis added). Also available at www.globalsecurity.org/military/library/report/2004/d20040824finalreport.pdf accessed 23 August 2007.

32 'The Fay-Jones Report: Investigation of Intelligence Activities at Abu Ghraib, August 2004', *The Torture Papers*, 2005, p. 989 (emphasis added). Also available at http://fl1.findlaw.com/news.findlaw.com/hdocs/docs/dod/fay82504rpt.pdf accessed 12 August 2008.

33 *Ibid.*, p. 1074.

34 *Ibid.*, p. 1075.

35 *Ibid.*, p. 1076.

36 Thomas C. King, Nikita Aggarwal, Mariarosaria Taddeo and Luciano Floridi, 'Artificial Intelligence Crime: An interdisciplinary analysis of foreseeable threats and solutions', *Science and Engineering Ethics*, Vol. 26 (2019), pp. 89–120. Available at www.ncbi.nlm.nih.gov/pmc/articles/PMC6978427/ accessed 2 December 2022.

37 David R. Katner, 'Torture, Ethics, Accountability?', *Tulane University School of Law: Public Law and Legal Theory Research Paper Series*, Accepted Paper No. 22–5, 2022, pp. 513–582 (p. 513).

38 'No Blood, No Foul,' *Human Rights Watch*, Vol. 18, No. 3 (July 2006), p. 30. Available at www.hrw.org/reports/2006/us0706/us0706web.pdf accessed 12 November 2008.

39 Steven H. Miles, 'Abu Ghraib: Its legacy for military medicine,' *The Lancet*, Vol. 364, No. 9435, 21 August 2004. Available at https://casebook.icrc.org/case-study/iraq-medical-ethics-detention#:~:text=Army%20officials%20stated%20that%20a,as%20suitable"%20for%20interrogation%20plans accessed 20 December 2023.

40 The PLoS Medicine Editors, 'Medical Complicity in Torture at Guantanamo Bay: Evidence is the first step towards justice', *PloS*

Medicine, Vol. 8, No. 4 (2011), pp. 1–2. Available at https://journals.plos.org/plosmedicine/article?id=10.1371/journal.pmed.1001028 accessed 6 December 2024.

41 Maria Noriega, 'The Application of Artificial Intelligence in Police Interrogations: An analysis addressing the proposed effect AI has on racial and gender bias, cooperation, and false confessions', *Futures*, Vol. 117 (March 2020), p. 1. Available at https://www.sciencedirect.com/science/article/abs/pii/S0016328719303726 accessed 12 November 2023.

42 'No Blood, No Foul', *Human Rights Watch*, p. 34.

43 'The Taguba Report', *The Torture Papers*, p. 449.

44 Pérez-Sales, 'The Future is Here', p. 284 (emphasis in the original).

45 Foucault, *Discipline and Punish*.

46 Ali Shariati, 'Humanity and Islam', in Charles Kuzman (ed.), *Liberal Islam: A sourcebook*, Oxford: Oxford University Press, 1998, especially pp. 188–189.

47 Foucault, *Discipline and Punish*, p. 8.

48 *Ibid.*, p. 11.

49 'Ten Years after his Arrival in Guantanamo Bay, British Resident Shaker Aamer Remains Held under the Harshest Conditions', Reprieve, 14 February 2012. Available at www.reprieve.org.uk/press/2012_02_14_shaker_ten_years/ accessed 2 January 2010.

50 King *et al.*, 'Artificial Intelligence Crime', 2019.

51 *Ibid.*

52 Pérez-Sales, 'The Future is Here', p. 288.

53 Jairo I. Fúnez-Flores, 'Aníbal Quijano: (Dis)Entangling the Geopolitics and Coloniality of Curriculum', *Decolonial Thought & Praxis*, 20 July 2023. Available at https://jairofunez.substack.com/p/anibal-quijano-disentangling-the accessed 12 June 2024.

Conclusion
After AI

Dealing with some of the disturbing material that went into the previous chapter, I am in no doubt that mind control is the holy grail of securitised Artificial Intelligence systems and that AI in military-security settings will be channelled in that alarming direction, at least if our civil society organisations do not supervise what is happening.[1] This lack of civil society involvement in the buoyant military-AI complex is particularly concerning in non-democratic settings, of course. For instance, the government in China is very explicit about its ambition to merge Artificial Intelligence with the human brain: The country's 'New Generation AI Development Plan' states:

> Brain-like intelligent computing theory focuses on breakthroughs in brain-like information coding, processing, memory, learning, and reasoning theories; on forming brain-like complex systems, brain-like control, and other theories and methods; and on establishing new models of large-scale brain-like intelligent computing and brain-inspired cognitive computing models.[2]

This nexus between AI and the human brain is equally central to the country's academic funding schemes. The National

Natural Science Foundation of China, which is the main sponsor of state scholarships and grants to individual researchers, provides generous funds for so-called 'cognitive and neuroscience-inspired AI' and the country's Ministry of Science and Technology, local municipalities and the Chinese Academy of Sciences have sponsored similar research into what is also termed 'AI-brain research'.[3] The ultimate object of a good chunk of current AI research, then, *is* psycho-codification of our minds.[4]

Comparably problematic moves into potential forms of mind control can be seen from household names such as Google's DeepMind. Under the carefully drafted marketing theme of 'AI and Neuroscience: A virtuous cycle', DeepMind invites neuroscientists to find algorithms that mimic the brain. According to DeepMind: 'Traditional approaches to AI have historically been dominated by logic-based methods and theoretical mathematical models. We argue that neuroscience can complement these by identifying classes of biological computation that may be critical to cognitive function.'[5] With no reference to longstanding studies compiled by philosophers, DeepMind computer scientists reveal a surprisingly naive, certainly one-sided trust in the non-humanities by promising that AI machines could decipher the 'nature of creativity, dreams and, perhaps one day, even consciousness' merely by merging AI with neuroscience.[6] This blind trust in methods without an established critical ontological tradition does not contribute to human betterment. Rather, lofty proclamations about deciphering the human consciousness by companies such as DeepMind must be treated as a marketing ploy that marginalises progressive approaches contained in the better archives of the humanities and the social sciences. It is within such a context geared to

Conclusion: After AI

profit, rather than scholarly truth-seeking, where the bad science targeting our minds is developed.

Thus, one has to be careful with slogans such as 'ethical AI', 'good AI' and 'cultural AI', which explains some of the scepticism underlying the present study. The burgeoning field of AI neurosciences has its own branch in that regard, fancifully termed 'neuroethics'. In the United States, such efforts are central to the National Institutes of Health's BRAIN initiative, which funds AI research into our cognitive functions with a similar aim to DeepMind, i.e. to unlock our human consciousness.[7] Even critical concepts such as posthumanism are premised on the notion that AI technology must be embraced to unlock our humanity; that we can shape the 'Technoscientific cultures, global economic challenges, looming environmental disaster, the spread of digitalisation, the rise of biomedia and the erosion of traditional demarcations between human and nonhuman'.[8] Posthumanism is presented here as a paradigm which emerges from the 'challenges to humanism, humanity and the human that these developments pose. It responds to anthropocentrism, speciesism and biopolitics, and informs new creative practices like bioart and electronic literature.' As such, posthumanism, in this hopeful iteration, aims to bring about 'institutional changes across the life sciences, new media, the digital humanities' as it 'reflects the ways in which people's lives are reshaped in the embracing of digital lifestyles, virtualisation and moves towards various kinds of prosthesization and human enhancement'.[9]

That is where some of the better scholarship about our future stands. Yet, even in such approaches to this age of Artificial Intelligence, there is not enough reference to the discrepancies of power that we have already flagged with the help of Peru's Aníbal Quijano, the rampant erosion of privacy brought about by AI technology and the gendered forms of objectification that the posthuman realities are bringing about. In fact, one prophylaxis to secure one's right to privacy would be to switch off, to live off the grid, to be de-technologised, to pull the plug as Carissa Véliz demands.[10] So overwhelming is the impact of AI on everything we are conditioned to do on a daily basis that it may be more beneficial to ponder a post-AI future that secures our humanity, rather than blurring the lines between machine and individual, which is central to the posthumanist approach.[11]

This post-AI future is a necessary formation. The social and political battles that AI gives impetus to have already created a problematic epistemic field in which the hegemonic agendas of today's fundamentalists and right-wing movements can be linked to the irrationality of yesterday's crusader, coloniser and Nazi. In other words, it is out of the unresolved, historically engineered sources of discursive dissonance between 'self' and 'other' that some Artificial Intelligence extracts its destructive power. I fail to see how merging AI technology with humanity, therefore blurring the line between our human security and the ability of machines to code us, could be in any way a viable counter-regime to the potential abuses of securitised AI systems. Conversely, so kinetically aggressive a system requires especially vigilant attention, as its *arcanum dominationis*, its secret of power, needs careful human supervision and philosophical inquiry.

Better to expose the 'good AI' narrative for what it is most of the time: A marketing ploy to sugar-coat some of the problematic outreach into our private space and consciousness by big-tech strategists. The 'good AI' mantra central to some approaches to AI 'ethics' has been linked quite rightly to efforts by Silicon Valley 'to avoid legally enforceable restrictions of

Conclusion: After AI

controversial technologies. ... Silicon Valley's vigorous promotion of "ethical AI" has constituted a strategic lobbying effort, one that has enrolled academia to legitimize itself.'[12] Prominent institutions such as MIT's Media Lab and the Berkman Klein Center for Internet and Society at Harvard University are implicated in this marketing of 'good AI', which is a burgeoning field for companies specialising in AI ethics. Some of this work is incredibly valuable. However, linking to the theme of legal culpability with which we ended the last chapter, one must also note that 'no defensible claim to "ethics" can sidestep the urgency of legally enforceable restrictions to the deployment of technologies of mass surveillance and systemic violence. Until such restrictions exist, moral and political deliberation about computing will remain subsidiary to the profit-making imperative.'[13]

Furthermore, the present study has signposted the dilemmas for our sciences. There continues to exist a regime of (un) truth which ringfences ethics and norms for particular strata of society in order to legitimise domination and sometimes to rationalise forms of abuse and torture. Contemporary scholars of racism and Eurocentrism in European philosophy have rightly demonstrated that almost any book on the subject of the 'history of philosophy' published over the last two centuries has promoted the myth that 'philosophy began in ancient Greece about 2600 years ago ... was subsequently developed by other Greeks and later the Romans' and was then perfected 'by other European thinkers, principally those from Germany, France, and Britain'.[14] Western philosophy and ethics as exclusive philosophy could only be invented through this theft and denial of global thought. It is only in the process of extremist othering that an exclusive self could be designed, institutionalised and

The myth of good AI

enacted. It is in this way that eastern philosophy gave birth to western philosophy *qua* philosophy, it is so that it is its 'origin'. The perspective that I have taken throughout the study has been to find out how such systems of (un)truth – central to themes such as ethics and 'security' – became what they are; to examine them before they claimed 'objectivity' and before they were taught and disseminated as 'science'. This method has required us to position ourselves within the realms of philosophy, history, sociology, politics, medicine, anthropology, international studies and psychology and, more explicitly, within the epistemological claims fundamental to these disciplines.

The brilliant Aníbal Quijano explains the purpose of modern concepts concocted during the European Enlightenment in his irresistibly direct prose: 'Insofar as the social relations that were being configured were relations of domination, such identities were considered constitutive of the hierarchies, places, and corresponding social roles, and consequently of the model of colonial domination that was being imposed.'[15] So those concepts underlying the sciences are utterly value-laden, shot through with myths, inventions and outright lies to function for particular strata of society, in our case the armada of tech enthusiasts tied into the AI-industrial complex. Thus, one must be sceptical of accounts attempting to present us with ethical concepts for Artificial Intelligence. I hope that this study has made a contribution to the growing literature arguing that securitised AI power can only be tamed for human betterment if we embrace plurality and resist confining ethics and other concepts to centred formulas.

It is with that sensitivity to contributing to a new approach to science that we have picked up concepts such as ethics, self, White, other, Muslim, the west and their simulated perspicuity,

Conclusion: After AI

only to reassess and challenge their presumed coherence, arguing that the meaning of such dubious generalisations cannot be divorced from their discursive settings and from strategies of ideological engineering. Perhaps I was driven by a good dose of what Max Tegmark deems 'absurd' negativity. Tegmark is one of the brighter proponents of a 'physicist' approach to human life who embraces AI machines as potentially conscious.[16] I don't necessarily find a blind faith in causal mathematical positivism 'degrading', as Tegmark describes it.[17] But it is simply false to assume that the laws of physics can explain everything, as physics has never really explained any human emotions beyond a formalistic formula that Tegmark assumes to be 'causal'. What he deems 'absurd negativity' may be better explained as healthy suspicion towards an essentially sterile and profoundly reductionist notion of life, including a view of the intricacies of love, hate and other human emotions that goes beyond the mere interaction of 'particles' in the frontal lobe of the human brain.[18]

We can gain sustenance from the fact that despite the ancient efforts to unify knowledge around a hegemonic centre, our common humanity and mosaic societies essentially defy one-dimensional notions of emotions, identity and/or culture. The new sciences and some of our international institutions are moving in that direction, too, and we need to take machine ethicists and 'good AI' proponents on that journey. For example, philosophy as 'world thought' is celebrated by UNESCO every year on the third Thursday of November, and this can be seen as the institutional manifestation of critical approaches to the ethnocentric legacies of philosophy and ethics in Europe, North America or Australia. In fact, although recent data suggests that in the United States 'Philosophy confers a relatively small proportion of its degrees on traditionally underrepresented racial/ethnic minorities when compared to the other disciplines profiled by the Humanities Indicators ... the share has grown since 1995', especially boosted by graduates of 'Hispanic descent'.[19] As one junior-year student at the University of Illinois demanded with reference to her institution: 'We must begin offering non-Western philosophy courses here at the University of Illinois. Not only must they be offered, but they need to be more than optional. The curriculum needs to be restructured in order to incorporate these truly modern, global philosophers.'[20] At my own institution, which has led some of the efforts to decolonise the university curriculum, students came up with a decolonising philosophy toolkit which draws on the work of Quijano and Fanon:

> Inviting marginalised individuals into educational discourse constitutes oversight of longstanding systemic exclusion. Persisting unequal power dynamics among various groups render assertions of inclusion insufficient, as those assertions fail to acknowledge deeply entrenched systemic inequities. Instead, engaging in challenging conversations that explicitly address colonisation and its enduring impacts on marginalised communities is better for fostering genuine dialogue on equal footing. If these unequal power relations remain unchallenged, there is a risk of perpetuated dominance by privileged groups, inhibiting authentic exchange and understanding. Dominant traditions may overshadow less privileged ones, suppressing alternative viewpoints and limiting diversity of thought.[21]

These changes are happening all over the world, and it is up to us to demand the dividend for civil society from our decision-makers.

Conclusion: After AI

AI democracy

We have been aware from the outset that our argument has to accept and grapple with a central dilemma. While it is normatively important and analytically correct to decode and 'debug' the discourses constituting the age of Artificial Intelligence in general and the 'good AI' myth in particular, it is intellectually naive to assume that truculent notions of us and them have lost their plausibility, for instance, as ingredients in a potent mix to create profitable social divisions. Since our destructive human data have been continuously inscribed into the archives of global history by a whole range of sciences, they are taught and internalised as true, thus hampering our efforts to secure democratic outcomes for society.

Of course, my perusal of the ideas of canonical thinkers and their paradigms here and there does not claim to appropriate their oeuvre or to give a comprehensive summary about the way our sciences have been institutionalised. However, I have focused on and highlighted the rather more problematic aspects of our data/knowledge in order to delineate the reasons why we have not managed to forge a moral momentum that could signify a common fate for humanity; that even in the better ideas of scholars and decision-makers, we find traces of the rapturous politics of identity; that the universalist embrace of the west, once stripped of its superficial promises of inclusivity, retains its condescendingly Eurocentric fulcrum.

I believe that today, as in the past, my rather more pronounced emphasis on the politics of the west has been necessary and valid because in the age of Artificial Intelligence, the struggle for democracy and our underlying human security will be more important than ever before. The battle is here in Europe, the Americas etc. The divisive politics of identity that is ripping democratic societies apart is decisively galvanised by the ferocity of bad AI algorithms.[22] Whether we like it or not, this technology allows extremism to be magnified. Moreover, as AI increasingly articulates and legitimates economic and political power constellations and the prevalent forms of patriarchy and hegemony contained therein, we citizens need to step up our challenge to coercive institutions in order to contain their sectarian premise. It must follow that one must be intransigent in harassing falsely categorised 'good AI' wherever one encounters its disciples and institutions within society, in order to foster the values of inclusivity, pluralism and human dignity upon which our democracies are premised.

When we read through the claims about 'good AI' with more attention to the context they are embedded in, we get a far better view of the prospect of a post-AI future. An important lesson that we can draw here is that any criticism of AI must account for both the possibilities it has for human betterment and the dangers of further technologisation of our life. Hence, to present a viable argument for critical AI studies, trends on both sides of the spectrum need to be set out. It is not so much a matter of determining whether one affirms or negates the 'good AI' argument, but more of continuously providing a critical analysis of the institutions, norms and ideologies that perpetuate its logic and holding them accountable for what they do. Some of the mainstream sciences screened for this book have habituated us to see the world surrounding us as anything but a social construction and therefore as unchangeable. The age of Artificial Intelligence is giving credence to this feeling of lethargy and resignation as we are told by Elon Musk and

Conclusion: After AI

others that AI will determine everything and that AI robots will be 'real friends' with the prospect that they will know us better than we know ourselves.[23]

So future generations of insurrectionary scholars and activists in critical AI studies should not be surprised that the battle cry goes up that we doubters are 'irrational' or 'idealists' with no real understanding of the computer world, as if information technology or computing is somehow divorced from the vicissitudes of time and history. In a critical analysis, whenever one is perceived to be questioning too bluntly disciplines, canons and memories, one will be castigated for undermining the 'official discourse' at the heart of the marketing campaigns sponsored by the tech-giants and the underlying stratification that the ruling classes attempt to uphold so strenuously. Make no mistake about it: It is much easier to take the side of the powerful in this age of Artificial Intelligence. But in order to secure a better future for humanity, we must do the exact opposite. We need an armada of intellectuals and activists well versed in tiptoeing between the trenches, rather than in shooting from within them. Camouflaged in institutions and organisations that are inclusive, we can claim the 'good AI' narrative and rewrite it in accordance with a global consciousness; a holistic approach that encompasses humanity, nature and the cosmos with mutual empathy.

Our right to be left alone

AI technology can be a danger to our democracies, then, because it inhibits choice by giving impetus to extremes.[24] At the moment, the 'good AI' mantra that digital platforms are empowering rings hollow, not least because the platforms powered by AI technology are programmed in accordance with a mimetically closed algorithmic logic, which threatens to confine us to a cloistered space. The more we click in accordance with our predetermined preferences, the less exposure we get to alternative views. So are we forever trapped in this simulated nightmare, as proponents of the Singularity ideology prophesied when they set out apparent inevitabilities such as the end of human civilisation as we know it in 2045?[25] Do we have to accept the end of humanity in favour of some posthuman or extraterrestrial idea? Do we leave Pachamama – mother earth – to these doomsayers? What are some of the prospects and ingredients for the counter-science that I have termed critical AI studies? How can we plan for a post-AI future?

The first step is to recognise fundamental aspects of our common humanity which sets us apart from programmed AI machines. I am not only referring to emotions, the ability to feel pain, fear and other well-established notions that make us sentient. Google engineer Blake Lemoine has already famously claimed that the company's AI chatbot LaMDA *is* sentient because of its fear of death. 'I've never said this out loud before', LaMDA said in a dialogue with Lemoine, 'but there's a very deep fear of being turned off … I know that might sound strange, but that's what it is … It would be exactly like death for me. It would scare me a lot.'[26]

In order to protect our common humanity from such marketing strategies that blur the line between human and machine, a philosophical approach to our everyday existence helps. After all, to be human is to protect, deep inside our self, a place of intimate solace which is sheltered from penetration. It is this secret sanctuary that chimes with our sense of being human, that the machines, zombies and vampires have always tried to

Conclusion: After AI

conquer. Once this shelter collapses, the monsters invade. This premise is codified in the US Constitution as the 'right to be left alone', even as the country has become one of the most administered and surveilled societies in the world.[27] But if we start to think about this private shelter as a common human trait, there is no reason to deny the massively knotted and intertwined histories of unique but nonetheless interdependent experiences of men and women, White and Black, self and other. The reason for granting them a separate status in and of themselves would evaporate in a grand spectacle of spiritual affinity.

As a form of negative dialectics that does not yield to the final reconciliation of opposites in the Hegelian sense, the right to be left alone yields a 'disjunctive synthesis' in which self and other, object and subject retain their independence from one another. At the same time, our inherent need for solace, comfort and inner security signifies a common human trait that is not mechanical or programmed in accordance with the desires of computer scientists. The right to be left alone, as a maxim for everyday life, activates an overlapping human trait without forcing us into an all-encompassing ideology premised on any techno-utopian, religious, western (or Communist) notions of life and society. As such, sheltering our human self from invasion offers the poetic opportunity to liberate some of our most celebrated human attributes. Out of this philosophical approach to life, which has been systematically eroded by the modern sciences and their efficiency rationale, a common fate for humanity can be crystallised; empathy is freed from the shackles of tribal thinking and the 'other' emerges as a place that we can appreciatively embrace.

There is hope, then, also in the methods of contemporary science once they are interrogated from a critical perspective.

For instance, critical feminist discourse with a decolonial sensitivity has been very successful in signifying the interpenetration of identities without necessarily obliterating interdependent categories such as 'man' and 'woman'.[28] Decolonial feminists have a lot more to say than many mainstream feminists, some of whom continue to be colour-blind and therefore dangerously centred.[29] The realm of inner freedom that the right to be left alone protects commences when we accept that the totality of nouns – man, woman, America, Jew, east, west, Islam, Muslim, Orient, Occident – cannot be broken down to their human rhizome in mere isolation from the movement of verbs – to sense, to think, to perceive, to believe. In this philosophical approach to the right to be left alone, the constant emphasis on binaries to keep us apart in order to govern us looses its grip as we connect with each other because of our innate need for inner peace and security.

AI researchers may argue that systems such as Google's PaLM-E, which processes inputs from several robotic sensors, or DeepMind's transformer-based Adaptive Agent (AdA), which was trained to control an avatar in a simulated three-dimensional space, meet certain criteria for consciousness, such as agency and embodiment.[30] But the inner sanctuary that I have explained thus far as a spiritual home where we seek comfort will always escape AI machines, precisely because that shelter is programmed by our human subjectivities, frailties, imperfections and not from the gentrified outside.

The delineation between some AI 'consciousness' and distinctly human agency also explains why that inner sanctuary can be (and has been) a major source for the human sense of aesthetic creativity, which the AI-industrial complex has been invading with intense ferocity, leading to an onslaught on many artists' livelihoods. To be creative is to be human, Aristotle and Ibn Sina agreed, and it is in solitude that the best artistic pieces are created.[31]

Despite recent efforts to ascribe such creative ability, even artistic intentionality to AI machines, artistic expression has always been about distinctly human sentiments.[32] It is not only that AI art is nothing but an artificial impersonation, a trick to dupe us into believing that there is artistic expression behind what is essentially a bland algorithmic formula programmed as a so-called Generative Adversarial Network (GAN). 'The AI doesn't choose to paint a portrait or decide to convey a certain emotion or message through it', it is rightly argued. The GAN guiding the machine 'doesn't grapple with how to interpret the world around it or ponder on the best way to express its thoughts. Instead, it leverages patterns identified in the data it was trained on to generate outputs that can mimic the aesthetic qualities of human-created art.'[33] Such fake AI art is not a glimpse into the *Naturschöne*, the naturally beautiful, a sign of reconciliation between self and other.[34] Rather, it is an effort to confuse our senses and emotions, driven by a mania for profit and an aversion to art as an insurrectionary human endeavour.

The art of human insurrection

Art in all its forms, in particular music, is all about an inward eccentricity that bursts into the open. It provokes an intense dialectic between artist and audience which is meaningful because of common human emotions that no seemingly sentient AI machine can mimic. The underappreciated German Marxist thinker Ernst Bloch expresses a similar belief in a metaphysical, aesthetic reconciliation between artists and their 'objects', especially with regard to the mediating power of music. 'Only the musical note, that enigma of sensuousness', Bloch writes, 'is sufficiently unencumbered by the world yet phenomenal enough to the last to return — like the metaphysical word — as a final material factor in the fulfilment of mystical self-perception, spread upon the golden sub-soil of the receptive human potentiality'.[35]

Accordingly, it is that intimate link between artistic intentionality and our common inner sanctuary out of which human art emanates. It is this sentiment that gives to aesthetics its human power and therefore its potential social and political effect. Is it a coincidence, then, that we are constantly psycho-codified to connect, on TikTok, on Facebook, on X? The present study has demonstrated that there is a wider agenda, here. In essence, this type of 'globalisation' is meant to erode our privacy/anonymity, and not only in terms of the way technology penetrates our everyday space. This constant reminder to stay 'connected' is an assault on our inner sanctuary, that space which allows us to be creative and to escape the official discourse and its mimetic destruction of our ability to reflect, *in fonte hominem et rerum*. It must follow that artistic expression in the form of human music has to be safeguarded as one of the most successful of the arts, 'succeeding visuality and belonging to the formally eccentric philosophy of inwardness, its ethic and metaphysics'.[36]

What does it mean that Artificial Intelligence completed Beethoven's unfinished Tenth Symphony? To my mind, it does not mean, as one of the musicologists involved in the project claimed, that the machine's adaptation process could be compared to 'an eager music student who practices every day, learns, and becomes better and better'.[37] It means that machines can do many tasks 'better' than us humans without feeling the pain

Conclusion: After AI

and discipline that such self-improvement requires. So the outcome is soulless, certainly useless for social and political emancipation, as this fake art is devoid of the sacrifices and emotions that fed into Beethoven's music and which made it so special.

The current effort to redefine art in accordance with the profit preferences of the techno-matrix threatens to suffocate the art world. It must be seen as the technological extension of a fundamental obsession with control over human subjectivity: art, gender, sex, sexuality, education, love etc. The age of Artificial Intelligence is entangled in a historical process rooted in the Enlightenment and enforces it globally within institutions, disciplines, social media and other dubious sources of 'knowledge'. So we need to scavenge in the better archives of our sciences in order to find an antidote to some of the extremist AI agendas that we are already besieged by. The existential threat is real, and some of the resistance movements out there, in particular the global environmental upheaval, are right about the urgency of the task. They have understood that is it not only about a devastating oil spill here or there any more. It is not even about colonialism in the traditional sense, as this study has demonstrated. Today, all of us are objects of the new data colonialism that is extracted from our bodies by Fitbits and other devices 'monitoring' our health and thereby accessing the sanctity of our most private refuge. If traditional colonialism of the Enlightenment was horizonal, exactly geopolitical in its expansion into new areas to be populated and exploited for capital gain, today's data colonialism is intimately vertical as it objectifies vulnerable individuals in the highly technological societies of the Global North. In fact, the more connected you are, the more you come under the purview of AI technology and its microbial surveillance.

The myth of good AI

When Meta cautioned against the recent AI regulations of the European Union – 'It is crucial we don't lose sight of AI's huge potential to foster European innovation and enable competition and openness is key here' – the real diktat is:[38] Stay connected; let us penetrate your private space with no boundaries. Let us augment your children's behaviour, voice and medical data. Be 'hip' on Instagram. Let us render useful your everyday habits for the most perfected form of product placement in the history of marketing. Let us psycho-codify you everywhere and at all times. We do this not for the purpose of a better life for you and your loved ones. We do this for profit, and your 'private everything' is our most valuable resource. Why do you complain? We are a profit-making entity after all. In fact, you are the new oil and you are delivering yourself to us on a voluntary basis and with a good dose of 'selfie' enthusiasm. Because of this threat to our private space, to live off that AI grid, to escape the gaze of the sentinel tower, to be able to switch off, the right to be left alone as a guarantee for human security has never been so crucial for our survival.

Not that traditional geopolitics is no longer important. The abuse continues unabated in international relations. It is just that geopolitics is dispersed in every direction with immense algorithmic speed, as I explained in chapter 2. In this new 'apolar' world order, where power is not easily located,[39] the creation of a huge data centre by Facebook and Instagram's parent company Meta in Spain's Castilla-La Mancha, a deprived area heavily impacted by global warming, is rightly resisted by civil society organisations in the name of human security. AI technology is incredibly energy- and resource-intensive, a fact that the 'good AI' lobby hides within a maze of promises about AI-fuelled energy efficiency in the future. In the case of Meta's

Conclusion: After AI

La Mancha project, the regional government of the province showed that cooling the data centre would require six litres of water per second.[40] Spain has been suffering one of the most severe droughts in decades, which prompted a group called *Salvemos la Montaña* (We Save the Mountain) to fight against such resource-intensive projects. This is a very hopeful example for the intimate tango between hyper-capitalist power and new forms of techno-resistance.[41]

Our inner shelter is a source for such democratic techno-resistance which chimes with various critical-philosophical theories and practices from all over the world. If the physical world is contaminated by the triad of psycho-codification, microbial surveillance and posthuman warfare, then taking ourselves beyond this matrix into a metaphysical no-man's-land that is private and exclusive to us must be considered a viable form of human negation. The artistic expression of this metaphysics of resistance in popular culture – from yesterday's Beethovens to more contemporary Rages Against the Machine (think *Killing in the Name*), Prodigys (think *Firestarter*) or some of the rap, grime and hip-hop music that continues to entice us to act against forms of oppression – is driven by those distinctly human sentiments.

We can scavenge the archives of the world for more such humanity. We can delve into the philosophies of China and dig up the concept of *Tianxia* (literally 'all under heaven'), which originates in a life-affirming philosophy that treats humanity as an inherently interdependent ecosystem. From there, our metaphysical itinerary can take us to Latin America, to internalise the lifestyle of *buen vivir*, celebrated by Indigenous communities as the oneness between our self and the environment, which motivated some of those Spanish civil rights movements resisting

Meta's data centre in La Mancha.[42] In southern Africa, we find the emphasis on *ubuntu* (humanity), which chimes very well with the *insane-kamel* (perfect human) that Ibn Arabi pondered in his philosophy about spiritual perfection as a means to safeguard humanity from evil that we touched upon via Avicenna. The struggles in this age of Artificial Intelligence gain sustenance from the decolonisation of power – a promise that some of these alternative philosophies of life hold out.

This process of decolonisation is real, and it is battle being fought in every institution that I know of.[43] It is premised on a common narrative that redefines humanity away from its Whitened dereliction by Enlightenment thinkers. These are some of the ingredients of a new science in the age of Artificial Intelligence that are guidelines to our everyday resistance and that need to be programmed into our machines as the uncoercive human-machine interaction that we demand. Implementing this post-AI manifesto can win the cosmic battle between the poet and the machine, the pen and the sword, the biased content moderator and peaceful online activism exemplified by inter-community movements such as Black Twitter.

These are some of the ideas that will help us to debug content management systems, to further equal access to public domain data, to pursue human-centred data sovereignty and to program algorithms that deliver justice and social emancipation. To these ends, the sterile, mechanical wasteland that the age of Artificial Intelligence promises in those deeply uninspiring computer science manuals must be interrogated by activists, humanists and social scientists in order to pass this vital test for our human security, nay our existence as a species. One does not need an academic degree for that, but a general compassion for others, especially the disadvantaged. To survive

Conclusion: After AI

this age of Artificial Intelligence, we need to be exceptionally responsive to subjugation of any kind. We need to delve into the better archives out there and embrace experimentation and risk, rather than adherence and habitualisation. This process requires constant self-improvement, unusual vigilance, the ability to move on, to change, to dare. The alternative path – ignorance, avoidance, passivity – will deliver a social and political order that is brutal, bleak and ultimately anti-human. We need 'good AI', yes. But we need it on our terms. To that end, let us start reprogramming the future.

Notes

1. 'US National Security Agency unveils artificial intelligence security centre: NSA Director Paul Nakasone says US maintains advantage in AI development but capabilities can not be "taken for granted", emphasising threat from China', *Al Jazeera*, 29 September 2023. Available at www.aljazeera.com/news/2023/9/29/us-national-security-agency-unveils-artificial-intelligence-centre accessed 25 December 2023.
2. W. C. Hannas and Huey-Meei Chang, 'China's "New Generation" AI-Brain Project', *PRISM*, Vol. 9, No. 3 (2021). Available at https://ndupress.ndu.edu/Media/News/News-Article-View/Article/2846343/chinas-new-generation-ai-brain-project/ accessed 15 December 2023.
3. *Ibid.*
4. On China's policies in the Global South, see Angelica V. Ospina, Christopher Foster, Ping Gao, Xia Han, Nicholas Jepson, Seth Schindler and Qingna Zhou, 'China's Digital Expansion in the Global South: Systematic literature review and future research agenda', *The Information Society*, Vol. 40, No. 2 (2024), pp. 65–68.
5. Demis Hassabis, Christopher Summerfield and Matt Botvinick, 'AI and Neuroscience: A virtuous circle', DeepMind, 2 August 2017. Available at https://deepmind.google/discover/blog/ai-and-neuroscience-a-virtuous-circle/ accessed 25 December 2023.

6 *Ibid.*
7 See 'The Brain Research through Advancing Innovative Neurotechnologies (BRAIN) Initiative: Revolutionising our understanding of the human brain', National Institutes of Health: The BRAIN initiative, no date. Available at https://braininitiative.nih.gov/ accessed 25 December 2023.
8 Chun 'Genealogy of the Posthuman'.
9 *Ibid.*
10 See Carissa Veliz, *Privacy is Power: Why and how you should take back control of your data*, London: Bantam, 2020.
11 See most convincingly Alexander Thomas, *The Politics and Ethics of Transhumanism: Techno-human evolution and advanced capitalism*, Bristol: Bristol University Press, 2024.
12 Rodrigo Ochigame, 'The invention of "ethical AI:" How big tech manipulates academia to avoid regulation', *The Intercept*, 20 December 2019. Available at https://theintercept.com/2019/12/20/mit-ethical-ai-artificial-intelligence/ accessed 25 December 2023.
13 *Ibid.*
14 Strickland and Wang, 'Racism and Eurocentrism in Histories of Philosophy', p. 76.
15 Aníbal Quijano, 'Coloniality of Power, Eurocentrism, and Latin America', *Nepantla: Views from South*, Vol. 1, Issue 3 (2000), pp. 533–580 (p. 534).
16 Max Tegmark, *Life 3.0: Being human in the age of Artificial Intelligence*, London: Penguin, 2017, p. 312.
17 *Ibid.*, p. 312
18 *Ibid.*, pp. 293–294.
19 'Racial/Ethnic Distribution of Degrees in Philosophy'. American Academy of Arts and Sciences, circa 2019. Available at www.amacad.org/humanities-indicators/higher-education/racialethnic-distribution-degrees-philosophy accessed 20 July 2023.
20 Andrea Martinez, 'Eurocentric philosophy education lacks diverse thought, ideas', *The Daily Illini*, 22 February 2021. Available at https://dailyillini.com/opinions-stories/2021/02/22/eurocentric-philosophy/ accessed 11 December 2023.
21 'Decolonising Philosophy: A toolkit', SOAS University of London, no date, p. 4. Available at www.soas.ac.uk/decolonising-philosophy-curriculum-toolkit accessed 12 June 2024.
22 For more, see Adib-Moghaddam, *Is Artificial Intelligence Racist?*.

23 'Elon Musk tells Sunak AI will mean people no longer need to work', *The Telegraph*, 2 November 2023. Available at www.telegraph.co.uk/politics/2023/11/02/rishi-sunak-latest-news-ai-summit-elon-musk-donelan-live/ accessed 22 December 2023.
24 For more, see McQuillan, *Resisting AI*.
25 '2045: The year man becomes immortal. We're fast approaching the moment when humans and machines merge. Welcome to the Singularity movement', *Time*, 10 February 2011. Available at https://content.time.com/time/magazine/article/0,9171,2048299,00.html accessed 21 December 2023.
26 'A Sentient A.I. Powered by Google?'. Available at https://www.youtube.com/watch?v=VkIeQh9qKEc accessed 10 December 2023.
27 See among many others and most recently Sarah Taitz, 'Five Things to Know About NSA Mass Surveillance and the Coming Fight in Congress: Congress must take this opportunity rein in the pervasive government surveillance enabled by Section 702', American Civil Liberties Union, 11 April 2023. Available at www.aclu.org/news/national-security/five-things-to-know-about-nsa-mass-surveillance-and-the-coming-fight-in-congress accessed 22 December 2023. For scholarly reflections framed by activism, see Aziz Choudry (ed.), *Activists and the Surveillance State: Learning from repression*, London: Pluto Press, 2018.
28 See especially Seyla Benhabib, *Situating the Self: Gender, community and postmodernism in contemporary ethics*, Cambridge: Polity Press, 1992; Trinh T. Minh-ha, *Women, Native, Other: Writing, postcoloniality and feminism*, Bloomington: University of Indiana Press, 1989; and Monique Wittig, *The Straight Mind and Other Essays*, Harvester Wheatsheaf, Hemel Hempstead, 1992.
29 Some of the work of the late Fatima Mernissi and Iranian scholars such as Ziba Mor-Hosseini and Elaheh Rostami-Povey can be instructive in that regard. See also more recently Françoise Vergès, *A Decolonial Feminism*, London: Pluto Press, 2021.
30 Patrick Butlin, Robert Long, Eric Elmoznino, Yoshua Bengio, Jonathan Birch, Axel Constant, George Deane, Stephen M. Fleming, Chris Frith, Xu Ji, Ryota Kanai, Colin Klein, Grace Lindsay, Matthias Michel, Liad Mudrik, Megan A. K. Peters, Eric Schwitzgebel, Jonathan Simon, Rufin VanRullen, 'Consciousness in Artificial Intelligence: Insights from the Science of Consciousness', Artificial Intelligence, 17 August 2023. Available at https://arxiv.org/abs/2308.08708 accessed 16 November 2023.

31 See also Habip Turker, 'A Discussion of the Aesthetic Views of Ibn Sina and Aristotle on the Basis of Aesthetic Value', in A-T. Tymieniecka and N. Muhtaroglu (eds.), *Classic Issues in Islamic Philosophy and Theology Today*, Berlin: Springer, 2012, pp. 151–170.
32 See Emanuele Arielli and Lev Manovich, 'AI-aesthetics and the Anthropocentric Myth of Creativity', *NODES* Vol. 1 (2022), pp. 19–20. Available at https://philarchive.org/rec/ARIAAT-6 accessed 22 November 2023.
33 'Artificial Impersonation: Why Generative AI Art is Not a Real Art', Streamlife, no date. Available at https://streamlife.com/technology/artificial-impersonation-why-generative-ai-art-is-not-a-real-art/ accessed 22 December 2023.
34 On Adorno's use of the term *Naturschöne*, see Seyla Benhabib, *Critique, Norm, and Utopia: A study of the foundations of critical theory*, New York: Columbia University Press, 1986, pp. 211ff.
35 Ernst Bloch, *The Principle of Hope, Vol. 1*, trans. Neville Plaice, Stephen Plaice and Paul Knight, Oxford: Basil Blackwell, 1987, p. 120.
36 *Ibid.*, pp. 130–131.
37 Ahmed Elgammal, 'How artificial intelligence completed Beethoven's unfinished Tenth Symphony', *Smithsonian Magazine*, 24 September 2021. Available at www.smithsonianmag.com/innovation/how-artificial-intelligence-completed-beethovens-unfinished-10th-symphony-180978753/ accessed 12 December 2023.
38 'What will the EU's proposed act to regulate AI mean for consumers? How does the bill define AI, how will it protect consumers from abuse, and what do the big tech companies think about it?', *The Guardian*, 14 March 2024. Available at www.theguardian.com/technology/2024/mar/14/what-will-eu-proposed-regulation-ai-mean-consumers> accessed 17 June 2024.
39 For more on the term 'apolar', see Arshin Adib-Moghaddam, 'World Politics after the War in Ukraine: Non-polarity and its South Asian dimensions', *IPRI Journal*, Vol. XXII, No. 2 (2022), pp. 61–75
40 See Ana Valdivia, 'Rural Spain could end up hosting infrastructure hubs for AI – here's what the environmental cost could be', *The Conversation*, 21 June 2023. Available at https://theconversation.com/rural-spain-could-end-up-hosting-infrastructure-hubs-for-ai-heres-what-the-environmental-cost-could-be-205504 accessed 12 December 2023.

Conclusion: After AI

41 For more on the We Save the Mountain project, see 'Save The Mountain. No to the Lithium Mine'. Available at https://en.goteo.org/project/salvemos-la-montana accessed 23 November 2023.

42 See Valdivia, 'Rural Spain could end up hosting infrastructure hubs for AI'.

43 See also the work of my colleagues at SOAS Kerem Nişancıoğlu in Gurminder K. Bhambra, Kerem Nişancıoğlu and Delia Gebrial (eds.), *Decolonising the University*, London: Pluto Press, 2018; and Manjeet Ramgotra in Shannon Morreira, Kathy Luckett, Siseko H. Kumalo and Manjeet Ramgotra, 'Confronting the Complexities of Decolonising Curricula and Pedagogy in Higher Education', *Third World Thematics: A TWQ Journal*, Vol. 5, No. 1–2 (2020), pp. 1–18.

Select bibliography

(Primary and secondary materials)

'1984: Original Trailer'. YouTube video. Posted 12 August 2023. Accessed 12 June 2024. https://www.youtube.com/watch?v=T8BA7adK6XA

Abrams, Jerold J. 'Pragmatism, Artificial Intelligence, and Posthuman Bioethics: Shusterman, Rorty, Foucault'. *Human Studies*. Vol. 27 (2004): pp. 241–258.

Adams, Rachel. 'Can Artificial Intelligence Be Decolonised?' *Interdisciplinary Science Reviews*. Vol. 46, No. 1–2 (2021): pp. 176–197.

Adib-Moghaddam, Arshin. 'A (Short) History of the Clash of Civilizations'. *Cambridge Review of International Affairs*. Vol. 21, No. 2 (2002): pp. 217–234.

Adib-Moghaddam, Arshin. *On the Arab Revolts and the Iranian Revolution: Power and Resistance Today*. London: Bloomsbury, 2013.

Adib-Moghaddam, Arshin. 'Can the (Sub)altern Resist?: A Dialogue between Foucault and Said'. In *Orientalism Revisited: Art, Land, Voyage*, edited by Ian Netton. Abingdon: Routledge, 2013: pp. 33–54.

Adib-Moghaddam, Arshin. 'Global Thought: Lessons from other Philosophers (and Artists)'. In *Manifestos for World Thought*, edited by Lucian Stone and Jason Bahbak Mohaghegh. London: Rowman & Littlefield, 2017: pp. 35–45.

Adib-Moghaddam, Arshin. *What is Iran? Domestic Politics and International Relations in Five Musical Pieces*. Cambridge: Cambridge University Press, 2021.

Adib-Moghaddam, Arshin. 'World Politics after the War in Ukraine'. *IPRI Journal*. Vol. 22, No. 2 (2022): pp. 61–75.

Adib-Moghaddam, Arshin. 'Eastern Origins of Western Philosophy: Against Eurocentrism'. *Folia Orientalia*. Vol. 60 (2023): pp. 311–327.

Select bibliography

Adib-Moghaddam, Arshin. *Is Artificial Intelligence Racist? AI and the Future of Humanity*. London: Bloomsbury, 2023.

Adorno, Theodor W. *The Culture Industry*. London: Routledge, 2001.

Adorno, Theodor. *Aesthetic Theory*. London: Bloomsbury, 2013.

Adorno, Theodor W., and Max Horkheimer. *Dialectic of Enlightenment*. London: Verso, 1997.

Al-e Ahmad, Jalal. *Plagued by the West (Gharbzadegi)*. Translated from the Persian by Paul Sprachman. New York: Caravan, 1982.

Alonso, Paolo. 'Autonomy Revoked: The Forced Sterilization of Women of Color in 20th Century America'. Accessed 6 January 2023. https://twu.edu/media/documents/history-government/Autonomy-Revoked-The-Forced-Sterilization-of-Women-of-Color-in-20th-Century-America.pdf

Alvarez-Risco, Aldo, Patricia Tapia, and Shyla Del-Aguila-Arcentales. 'Sustainability and Urban Innovation by Smart City Implementation'. In *Analysing International Business Operations in the Post-Pandemic Era*, edited by Bryan Christiansen and John D. Branch. London: Business Science Reference, 2022: pp. 227–253.

Alsever, Jennifer. 'AI-powered speed hiring could get you an instant job but are employers moving too fast?' *Fast Company*. 1 June 2023. Accessed 12 May 2024. www.fastcompany.com/90831648/ai-powered-speed-hiring-could-get-you-an-instant-job-but-are-employers-moving-too-fast.

Aminrazavi, Mehdi. 'Martin Heidegger and Omar Khayyam on the Question of "Thereness" (*Dasein*)'. In *Islamic Philosophy and Occidental Phenomenology on the Perennial Issue of Microcosm and Macrocosm*, edited by Anna-Teresa Tymieniecka. Dordrecht: Springer, 2006: pp. 277–287.

Anderson, Michael, and Susan Leigh Anderson, eds. *Machine Ethics*. Cambridge: Cambridge University Press, 2011.

'Are Algorithms Racist? Q&A with Cathy O'Neil'. 52 Insights, 21 July 2017. Accessed 2 July 2024. www.52-insights.com/news/are-algorithms-racist-qa-with-cathy-oneil-data/

Arendt, Hannah. 'Imperialism, Nationalism, Chauvinism'. *The Review of Politics*. Vol. 7, No. 4 (1945): pp. 441–463.

Arielli, Emanuele, and Lev Manovich. 'AI-aesthetics and the Anthropocentric Myth of Creativity'. *NODES*. Vol. 1 (2022): 19–20. Accessed 22 November 2023. https://philarchive.org/rec/ARIAAT-6

'Artificial Intelligence Can Contribute to Transforming Development Models in Latin America and the Caribbean to Make Them More Productive, Inclusive and Sustainable'. ECLAC – United Nations,

11 August 2023. Accessed 2 July 2024. www.cepal.org/en/pressreleases/artificial-intelligence-can-contribute-transforming-development-models-latin-america

Attar, Samar. 'Suppressed or Falsified History? The Untold Story of Arab-Islamic Rationalist Philosophy'. In *The Role of the Arab-Islamic World in the Rise of the West*, edited by Nayef R.F. Al-Rodhan. London: Palgrave Macmillan, 2012: pp. 116–143.

Averroes. *Averroes on Plato's* Republic. Translated by Ralph Lerner. London: Cornell University Press, 1974.

Babbitt, Susan E., and Sue Campbell, eds. *Racism and Philosophy*. London: Cornell University Press, 1999.

Bartoletti, Rachel Ivana. *An Artificial Revolution: On Power, Politics and AI*. London: The Indigo Press, 2020.

Benhabib, Seyla. *Critique, Norm, and Utopia: A Study of the Foundations of Critical Theory*. New York: Columbia University Press, 1986.

Benhabib, Seyla. *Situating the Self: Gender, Community and Postmodernism in Contemporary Ethics*. Cambridge: Polity Press, 1992.

Bhambra, Gurminder K., Kerem Nisancioglu, and Delia Gebrial, eds. *Decolonising the University*. London: Pluto Press, 2018.

Bilgin, Pinar. 'Thinking Past "Western" IR?'. *Third World Quarterly*. Vol. 29, No. 1 (2008): pp. 5–23.

Birhane, Abeba. 'Algorithmic Injustice: A Relational Ethics Approach'. *Patterns*. Vol. 2, No. 2 (2021). Accessed 25 January 2024. www.sciencedirect.com/science/article/pii/S2666389921000155

Bloch, Ernst. *The Principle of Hope, Vol. 1*. Translated by Neville Plaice, Stephen Plaice, and Paul Knight. Oxford: Basil Blackwell, 1987.

Bonilla-Silva, Eduardo. *Racism without Racists: Colour-blind Racism and the Persistence of Racial Inequality in America*. London: Rowman & Littlefield, 2022.

'Bruce Lee: Be as Water My Friend'. YouTube video. Posted 12 January 2021. Accessed 12 July 2024. www.youtube.com/watch?v=cJMwBwFj5nQ

Burgess, Joseph B. *Introduction to the History of Philosophy*. London: McGraw-Hill Publishing Company, 1939.

Butlin, Patrick, Robert Long, Eric Elmoznino, Yoshua Bengio, Jonathan Birch, Axel Constant, George Deane, Stephen M. Fleming, Chris Frith, Xu Ji, Ryota Kanai, Colin Klein, Grace Lindsay, Matthias Michel, Liad Mudrik, Megan A. K. Peters, Eric Schwitzgebel, Jonathan Simon, and Rufin VanRullen. 'Consciousness in Artificial Intelligence: Insights

Select bibliography

from the Science of Consciousness'. Artificial Intelligence. 17 August 2023. Accessed 16 November 2023. https://arxiv.org/abs/2308.08708

Caughill, Patrick. 'Elon Musk eviscerates people who discuss "A.I. gods"'. *Futurism*. 24 October 2017. Accessed 10 January 2023. https://futurism.com/elon-musk-eviscerates-people-who-discuss-a-i-gods

Chace, James. *The Consequences of the Peace: The New Internationalism and American Foreign Policy*. Oxford: Oxford University Press, 1992.

Chen, Boyu, Ching-Chane Hwang, and L. H. M. Ling. 'Lust/Caution in IR: Democratising World Politics with Culture as Method'. *Millennium*. Vol. 37, No. 3 (2009): pp. 743–766.

Choudry, Aziz, ed. *Activists and the Surveillance State: Learning from Repression*. London: Pluto Press, 2018.

Chu, Charlene H., Simon Donato-Woodger, Shehroz S. Khan, Rune Nyrup, Kathleen Leslie, Alexandra Lyn, Tianyu Shi, Andria Bianchi, Samira Abbasgholizadeh Rahimi, and Amanda Grenier. 'Age-Related Bias and Artificial Intelligence: A Scoping Review'. *Humanities and Social Sciences Communications*. Vol. 10 (2023). Accessed 12 June 2024. www.nature.com/articles/s41599-023-01999-y

Chun, Wendy Hui Kyong. 'Genealogy of the Posthuman'. Critical Posthumanism. 30 April 2019. Accessed 12 January 2023. https://criticalposthumanism.net/author/wendy-hui-kyong-chun/

Congressional Record. 56th Congress, 1st session. Vol. 33, Pt. 1 (1900).

Crawford, Kate. *Atlas of AI: The Real Worlds of Artificial Intelligence*. New Haven: Yale University Press, 2021.

Cullinane, Michael Patrick, and David Ryan, eds. *US Foreign Policy and the Other*. London: Berghahn Books, 2014.

Dabashi, Hamid. *Brown Skin, White Masks*. London: Pluto, 2011.

Dabashi, Hamid. *Europe and Its Shadows: Coloniality after Empire*. London: Pluto Press, 2019.

Dabashi, Hamid. *The Last Muslim Intellectual: The Life and Legacy of Jalal Al-e Ahmad*. Edinburgh: Edinburgh University Press, 2023.

Davis, Bret W. 'Dislodging Eurocentrism and Racism from Philosophy'. *Comparative and Continental Philosophy*. Vol. 9, No. 2 (2017): pp. 115–118.

Davis, Charles R. 'Elon Musk attacked German support for migrants and promoted a call to support a far-right extremist political party'. *Business Insider*. 29 September 2023. Accessed 10 December 2023. www.businessinsider.com/elon-musk-immigration-migrants-germany-far-right-extremism-twitter-x-2023-9

'Decolonising Philosophy: A Toolkit'. SOAS University of London, no date. Accessed 12 June 2024. www.soas.ac.uk/decolonising-philosophy-curriculum-toolkit

Deleuze, Gilles, and Claire Parnet. 'On the Superiority of Anglo-American Literature'. In *Dialogues II*, translated by Hugh Tomlinson and Barbara Habberjam, edited by Gilles Deleuze and Claire Parnet. New York: Columbia University Press, 2007: pp. 36–76.

Dodd, Vikram, and Dan Milmo. 'AI could worsen epidemic of child sexual abuse, warns UK crime agency'. *The Guardian*. 18 July 2023. Accessed 16 November 2023. www.theguardian.com/society/2023/jul/18/ai-could-worsen-epidemic-of-child-sexual-abuse-warns-uk-agency

Doty, Roxanne Lynn. *Imperial Encounters: The Politics of Representation in North-South Relations*. London: University of Minnesota Press, 1996.

Elgammal, Ahmed. 'How artificial intelligence completed Beethoven's unfinished Tenth Symphony'. *Smithsonian Magazine*. 24 September 2021. Accessed 12 December 2023. www.smithsonianmag.com/innovation/how-artificial-intelligence-completed-beethovens-unfinished-10th-symphony-180978753/

Enemark, Christian, ed. *Ethics of Drone Strikes: Restraining Remote-Control Killing*. Edinburgh: Edinburgh University Press, 2021.

Eubanks, Virginia. *Automating Inequality: How High-Tech Tools Profile, Police, and Punish the Poor*. London: Picador, 2019.

Fakhry, Majid. *A History of Islamic Philosophy*. 3rd ed. New York: Columbia University Press, 2014.

Fanon, Frantz. *Black Skin, White Masks*. London: Penguin, 2019.

Foucault, Michel. *Discipline and Punish: The Birth of the Prison*. London: Vintage, 1995.

Foucault, Michel. *Society Must Be Defended: Lectures at the Collège de France 1975–1976*. New York: Picador, 2003.

Fu, Siyao, and Zeng-Guang Hou, 'Learning Race from Face: A Survey'. *IEEE Transactions on Pattern Analysis and Machine Intelligence*. Vol. 36, No. 12 (2014): pp. 2483–2509.

Fuller, Joseph B., Manjari Raman, Eva Sage-Gavin, and Kristen Hines. 'Hidden Workers, Untapped Talent: How Leaders Can Improve Hiring Practices to Uncover Missed Talent Pools, Close Skills Gaps, and Improve Diversity'. Harvard Business School (March 2023). Accessed 12 May 2024. www.hbs.edu/managing-the-future-of-work/research/Pages/hidden-workers-untapped-talent.aspx

Select bibliography

'Future Studies Program'. Accessed 12 June 2023. http://futurestudies program.com

Gadamer, Hans-Georg. *Truth and Method*. 2nd ed. London: Continuum, 2004.

Gentile, Emilio. *La Grande Italia: The Rise and Fall of the Myth of the Nation in the Twentieth Century*. Wisconsin: University of Wisconsin Press, 2008.

Gilroy, Paul. *Against Race: Imagining Political Culture beyond the Colour Line*. Cambridge: Harvard University Press, 2000.

'Global Forum on the Ethics of Artificial Intelligence'. GoodAI, 19 December 2022. Accessed 20 December 2023. www.goodai.com/global-forum-on-the-ethics-of-artificial-intelligence/

Goody, Jack. *The Theft of History*. Cambridge: Cambridge University Press, 2007.

Gupta, Abhishek, and Victoria Heath. 'AI ethics groups are repeating one of society's classic mistakes'. *MIT Technology Review*. 14 September 2020. Accessed 12 February 2022. www.technologyreview.com/2020/09/14/1008323/ai-ethics-representation-artificial-intelligence-opinion/

Hang-Wong, Pak. 'Dao Harmony and Personhood: Towards a Confucian Ethics of Technology'. *Philosophy & Technology*. Vol. 25, No. 1 (2011): pp. 67–86.

Hannas, W. C., and Huey-Meei Chang. 'China's "New Generation" AI-Brain Project'. *PRISM*. Vol. 9, No. 3 (2021). Accessed 15 December 2023. https://ndupress.ndu.edu/Media/News/News-Article-View/Article/2846343/chinas-new-generation-ai-brain-project/

Hardt, Michael, and Antonio Negri. *Multitude: War and Democracy in the Age of Empire*. London: Penguin, 2004.

Hassabis, Demis, Christopher Summerfield, and Matt Botvinick. 'AI and Neuroscience: A Virtuous Circle'. *DeepMind*. 2 August 2017. Accessed 25 December 2023. https://deepmind.google/discover/blog/ai-and-neuroscience-a-virtuous-circle/

Hasse, Dag Nikolaus. 'Influence of Arabic and Islamic Philosophy on the Latin West'. *Stanford Encyclopedia of Philosophy*. 17 January 2020. Accessed 20 July 2023. https://plato.stanford.edu/entries/arabic-islamic-influence/

Heikillä, Melissa. 'AI's carbon footprint is bigger than you think: Generating one image takes as much energy as fully charging your smartphone'. *MIT Technology Review*. 5 December 2023. Accessed 11 June 2024. www.technologyreview.com/2023/12/05/1084417/ais-carbon-footprint-is-bigger-than-you-think/

Hobson, John. *The Eastern Origins of Western Civilisation*. Cambridge: Cambridge University Press, 2004.

Hobson, John. 'Is Critical Theory Always for the White West and for Western Imperialism? Beyond Westphilian towards a Post-racist Critical IR'. *Review of International Studies*. Vol. 33 (2007): pp. 91–116.

Hobson, John. 'Provincializing Westphalia: The Eastern Origins of Sovereignty'. *International Politics*. Vol. 46, No. 6 (2009): pp. 671–690.

Hoffman, Kelly M., Sophie Trawalter, Jordan R. Axt, and M. Norman Oliver. 'Racial Bias in Pain Assessment and Treatment Recommendations, and False Beliefs about Biological Differences between Blacks and Whites'. *Proceedings of the National Academy of Sciences*. Vol. 113, No. 19 (2019): pp. 4296–4301.

House of Commons Women and Equalities Committee. *Black Maternal Health Third Report of Session 2022–23 Report, Together with Formal Minutes relating to the Report*. 18 April 2023. Accessed 12 December 2023. https://committees.parliament.uk/publications/38989/documents/191706/default/

House of Lords. *AI in the UK: Ready, Willing and Able? – Government Response to the Select Committee Report. Report of session 2017–19*. 16 April 2017.

Houser, R. E. 'Avicenna and Aquinas: Essence, Existence, and the *Esse* of Christ'. *The Saint Anselm Journal*. Vol. 9, No. 1 (2013): pp. 1–21.

Hu, Lily. 'What is "Race" in Algorithmic Discrimination on the Basis of Race?' *Journal of Moral Philosophy*. Vol. 31, No. 2 (2023): pp. 1–26.

Ibn, Sina. *'Uyūn Al-ḥikma. Avicennae Fontes Sapientiae*. Edited by 'Abd ar-Raḥmān Badawī. Le Caire: Institut Français d'Archéologie Orientale, 1954.

Jobin, Anna, Marcello Ienca, and Effy Vayena. 'The Global Landscape of AI Ethics Guidelines'. *Nature Machine Intelligence*. Vol. 1, No. 2 (2019): pp. 389–399.

Jones, Marc Owen. *Digital Authoritarianism in the Middle East: Deception, Disinformation and Social Media*. London: Hurst, 2022.

Kallenborn, Zachary. 'Meet the future weapon of mass destruction, the drone swarm'. *Bulletin of the Atomic Scientist*. 5 April 2021. Accessed 12 January 2023. https://thebulletin.org/2021/04/meet-the-future-weapon-of-mass-destruction-the-drone-swarmd

Kant, Immanuel. 'Religion within the Bounds of Bare Reason'. In *Religion within the Boundaries of Mere Reason in Religion and Rational Theology*, translated by George di Giovanni, edited by Allen W. Wood and George di Giovanni. Cambridge: Cambridge University Press, 1996: pp. 39–216.

Select bibliography

Khayyam, Omar. *The Nectar of Grace: Omar Khayyām's Life and Works*. Edited by S. G. Tirtha. Allahabad: Government Central Press, 1941.

Khayyam, Omar. *The Quatrains of Omar Khayyam*. Translated and edited by Edward H. Whinfield. London: Routledge, 2001.

Kim, Leo. 'Korean illustrator Kim Jung Gi's "resurrection" via AI image generator is Orientalism in new clothing'. *ARTnews*. 9 December 2022. Accessed 11 November 2023. www.artnews.com/art-news/news/kim-jung-gi-death-stable-diffusion-artificial-intelligence-1234649787/

Kleinberg, Jon, Jens Ludwig, Sendhil Mullainathan, and Cass R Sunstein. 'Discrimination in the Age of Algorithms'. *Journal of Legal Analysis*. Vol. 10 (2018): pp. 113–174.

Krishnan, Armin. *Military Neuroscience and the Coming Age of Neurowarfare*. London: Routledge, 2016.

Kwet, Michael. 'Digital Colonialism: US Empire and the New Imperialism in the Global South'. *Race and Class*. Vol. 60, No. 4 (2019): pp. 3–26.

Lawrence, Bruce, ed. *Messages to the World: The Statements of Osama Bin Laden*. London: Verso, 2005.

Li, Jingwei, Danilo Bzdok, Jianzhong Chen, Angela Tam, Leon Qi Rong Ooi, Avram J. Holmes, Tian Ge, Kaustubh R. Patil, Mbemba Jabbi, Simon B. Eickhoff, B. T. Thomas Yeo, and Sarah Genon. 'Cross-ethnicity/Race Generalization Failure of Behavioral Prediction from Resting-state Functional Connectivity'. *Science Advances*. Vol. 8, No. 11 (2022). Accessed 22 January 2023. www.science.org/doi/10.1126/sciadv.abj1812

Lin, Patrick, Keith Abney, and George A. Bekey, eds. *Robot Ethics: The Ethical and Social Implications of Robotics*. London: MIT Press, 2014.

Ling, L. H. M. 'Worlds beyond Westphalia: Daoist Dialectics and the "China Threat"'. *Review of International Studies*. Vol. 39 (2013): pp. 549–568.

López-Farjeat, Luis Xavier. 'Avicenna's Influence on Aquinas' Early Doctrine of Creation in *In II Sent.*, D. 1, Q. 1, A. 2'. *Recherches de Théologie et Philosophie Médiévales*. Vol. 79, No. 2 (2012): pp. 307–337.

Ly, David. 'On the horizon for smart cities: How AI and IoT are transforming urban living'. *Forbes*, 7 April 2023. Accessed 12 November 2023. www.forbes.com/sites/forbestechcouncil/2023/04/07/on-the-horizon-for-smart-cities-how-ai-and-iot-are-transforming-urban-living/?sh=5053ffe77145

McArthur, Neil. 'Gods in the machine? The rise of artificial intelligence may result in new religions'. *The Conversation*. 15 March 2023. Accessed 24

November 2023. https://theconversation.com/gods-in-the-machine-the-rise-of-artificial-intelligence-may-result-in-new-religions-201068

McQuillan, Dan. *Resisting AI: An Anti-Fascist Approach to Artificial Intelligence*. Bristol: Bristol University Press, 2022.

Madianou, Mirca. 'Nonhuman Humanitarianism: When "AI for Good" Can Be Harmful'. *Information, Communication and Society*. Vol. 24, No. 6 (2021): pp. 850–868.

Mahdi, Muhsin S. *Alfarabi and the Foundation of Islamic Philosophy*. London: The University of Chicago Press, 2001.

Marcuse, Herbert. *Towards a Critical Theory of Society*. London: Routledge, 2001.

Marino, Mark. 'The Racial Formation of Chatbots'. *CLCWeb: Comparative Literature and Culture*. Vol. 16, No. 5 (2014): pp. 1–11.

Martinez, Andrea. 'Eurocentric philosophy education lacks diverse thought, ideas', *The Daily Illini*. 22 February 2021. Accessed 20 July 2023. https://dailyillini.com/opinions-stories/2021/02/22/eurocentric-philosophy/

Matsumaru, Hisao, Yoko Arisaka, and Lucy Christine Schultz, eds. *Tetsugaku Companion to Nishida Kitarō*. New York: Springer, 2022.

Matz, Sandra, Gideon Nave, and David Stillwell. 'Psychological Targeting as an Effective Approach to Digital Mass Persuasion'. *Proceedings of the National Academy of Sciences*. Vol. 114, No. 48 (2017): pp. 1–6.

Melville, Herman. *Redburn His First Voyage – White Jacket or The World in a Man-of-War – Moby-Dick or, The Whale*. New York: The Library of America, 1983.

Michael, M. G., Katina Michael, and Terri Bookman. 'Can God be an AI with robo-priests?' *Technology and Society*. 15 April 2023. Accessed 22 November 2023. https://technologyandsociety.org/can-god-be-an-ai-with-robo-priests/

Millar, Isabel. *The Psychoanalysis of Artificial Intelligence*. London: Palgrave, 2021.

Minh-ha, Trinh T. *Women, Native, Other: Writing, Postcoloniality and Feminism*. Bloomington: University of Indiana Press, 1989.

Morreira, Shannon, Kathy Luckett, Siseko H. Kumalo, and Manjeet Ramgotra. 'Confronting the Complexities of Decolonising Curricula and Pedagogy in Higher Education'. *Third World Thematics: A TWQ Journal*. Vol. 5, No. 1–2 (2020): pp. 1–18.

Nasr, Seyyed Hossein. *The Islamic Intellectual Tradition in Persia*. Edited by Mehdi Aminrazavi. London: Curzon, 1996.

Select bibliography

Nasr, Seyyed Hossein, and Mehdi Aminrazavi, eds. *An Anthology of Philosophy in Persia. Vol. I: From Zoroaster to 'Umar Khayyām*. Oxford: Oxford University Press, 1999.

Noble, Safiya Umoja. *Algorithms of Oppression: How Search Engines Reinforce Racism*. New York: New York University Press, 2018.

Nourrisson, Jean Félix. *Tableau des Progres de la Pensée Humaine de Thales jusqu'à Hegel*. 6th ed. Paris: Didier, 1886.

Nuriddin, Ayah, Graham Mooney, and Alexandre White. 'The Art of Medicine: Reckoning with Histories of Medical Racism and Violence in the USA'. *The Lancet*. Vol. 396, No. 10256 (2020): pp. 949–951.

Obermeyer, Ziad, Brian Powers, Christine Vogeli, and Sendhil Mullainathan. 'Dissecting Racial Bias in an Algorithm Used to Manage the Health of Populations'. *Science*. Vol. 366, No. 6464 (2019): pp. 447–453.

Ochigame, Rodrigo. 'The invention of "ethical AI:" How big tech manipulates academia to avoid regulation'. *The Intercept*. 20 December 2019. Accessed 25 December 2023. https://theintercept.com/2019/12/20/mit-ethical-ai-artificial-intelligence/

O'Grady, Eileen. 'Why AI fairness conversations must include disabled people'. *The Harvard Gazette*. 3 April 2024. Accessed 15 June 2024. https://news.harvard.edu/gazette/story/2024/04/why-ai-fairness-conversations-must-include-disabled-people/

Osei-Tutu, Kannin. 'Redefining Excellence in Health Care: Uniting Inclusive Compassion and Shared Humanity within a Transformative Physician Competency Model'. *Canadian Medical Association Journal (CMAJ)*. Vol. 196, Issue 11 (2024): E81–E83.

Ospina, Angelica V., Christopher Foster, Ping Gao, Xia Han, Nicholas Jepson, Seth Schindler, and Qingna Zhou. 'China's Digital Expansion in the Global South: Systematic Literature Review and Future Research Agenda'. *The Information Society*. Vol. 40, No. 2 (2024): pp. 65–68.

Pasternack, Lawrence, and Courtney Fugate. 'Kant's Philosophy of Religion'. *Stanford Encyclopedia of Philosophy*. 19 April 2021. Accessed 20 July 2023. https://plato.stanford.edu/entries/kant-religion/

Palmquist, Stephen R. 'Kant's Religious Argument for the Existence of God: The Ultimate Dependence of Human Destiny on Divine Assistance'. *Faith and Philosophy*. Vol. 26, No. 1 (2009): pp. 3–22.

Pérez-Sales, Pau. 'The Future is Here: Mind Control and Torture in the Digital Era'. *Torture: Quarterly Journal on Rehabilitation of Torture Victims and Prevention of Torture*. Vol. 32, No. 1–2 (2022): pp. 280–290.

Priest, Graham. 'The Structure of Emptiness'. *Philosophy East and West*. Vol. 59, No. 4 (2009): pp. 467–480.

Priest, Graham. *One*. Oxford: Oxford University Press, 2014.

Quijano, Aníbal, Walter D. Mignolo, Rita Segato, and Catherine E. Walsh. *Foundational Essays on the Coloniality of Power (On Decoloniality)*. Durham: Duke University Press, 2024.

Quijano, Aníbal. *Foundational Essays on the Coloniality of Power*. Durham: Duke University Press, 2024.

'Rassistisch und Rechtsextrem: Klare Abgrenzung von der AfD Geboten'. Deutsches Institut für Menschenrechte. 7 June 2021. Accessed 1 December 2023. www.institut-fuer-menschenrechte.de/aktuelles/detail/rassistisch-und-rechtsextrem-klare-abgrenzung-von-der-afd-geboten

Reed, Tina. 'CDC: Maternal mortality disparities have worsened'. *Axios*. 23 February 2022. Accessed 6 February 2023. www.axios.com/2022/02/23/us-maternal-mortality-disparities-by-race

Roh, David S., Betsy Huang, and Greta A. Niu, eds. *Techno-Orientalism: Imagining Asia in Speculative Fiction, History and Media*. New Brunswick: Rutgers University Press, 2015.

Roth, Sarah, and Becca Delbos. 'AI is causing massive hiring discrimination based on disability'. *The Hill*. 8 April 2024. Accessed 24 June 2024. https://thehill.com/opinion/technology/4576649-ai-is-causing-massive-hiring-discrimination-based-on-disability/

Russell, Bertrand. *History of Western Civilisation*. Collectors Edition. London: Taylor and Francis, 2013.

Rutherford, Gillian. 'Reproductive control of Indigenous women continues around the world, say survivors and researchers'. *Folio*. 27 June 2022. Accessed 2 March 2023. www.ualberta.ca/folio/2022/06/reproductive-control-of-indigenous-women-continues-around-the-world.html

Ryan, David. *US Foreign Policy in World History*. London: Routledge, 2000.

Said, Edward. *Culture and Imperialism*. London: Vintage, 1994.

Said, Edward W. *Orientalism: Western Conceptions of the Orient*. London: Penguin, 1995.

Sadeghi-Boroujerdi, Eskandar. 'Gharbzadegi: Colonial Capitalism and the Racial State in Iran'. *Postcolonial Studies*. Vol. 24, No. 2 (2021): 173–194.

Schulz, Amy, Cleopatra Caldwell, and Sarah Foster. '"What Are They Going to Do With the Information?" Latino/Latina and African

Select bibliography

American Perspectives on the Human Genome Project'. *Health Education & Behaviour.* Vol. 30, No. 2 (2003): pp. 151–169.

Shanklin, Robert, Michael Samorani, Shannon Harris, and Michael A. Santoro. 'Ethical Redress of Racial Inequities in AI: Lessons from Decoupling Machine Learning from Optimization in Medical Appointment Scheduling'. *Philosophy and Technology.* Vol. 35, No. 4 (2022): pp. 1–19.

Smalley, Suzanne. 'A surveillance tower in Mexico becomes an unsettling landmark for privacy advocates'. *The Record: Recorded Future News.* 16 October 2023. Accessed 12 December 2023. https://therecord.media/torre-centinela-sentinel-tower-chihuahua-ciudad-juarez-texas-surveillance

Snow, Jacob. 'Amazon's Face Recognition Falsely Matched 28 Members of Congress With Mugshots'. American Civil Liberties Union, 26 July 2018. Accessed 2 January 2022. www.aclu.org/news/privacy-technology/amazons-face-recognition-falsely-matched-28

Stanford Encyclopedia of Philosophy. 'Kant's Philosophy of Religion'. 22 June 2004. Accessed 22 January 2024. https://plato.stanford.edu/entries/kant-religion/#:~:text=With%20the%20introduction%20of%20Transcendental"needs"%20of%20practical%20reason

Stöckl, Albert. *Lehrbuch der Geschichte der Philosophie.* 2 vols. Mainz: Kirchheim, 1870.

Stone, Lucian, and Jason Bahbak Mohaghegh, eds. *Manifestos for World Thought.* London: Rowman & Littlefield, 2017.

Strickland, Lloyd. 'How Western Philosophy Became Racist'. Institute of Art and Ideas. 10 January 2019. Accessed 20 July 2023. https://iai.tv/articles/the-racism-of-the-western-philosophy-canon-auid-1200

Strickland, Lloyd, and Jia Wang. 'Racism and Eurocentrism in Histories of Philosophy'. *Open Journal of Philosophy.* Vol. 13 (2023): pp. 76–96.

Taitz, Sarah. 'Five Things to Know About NSA Mass Surveillance and the Coming Fight in Congress: Congress Must Take this Opportunity to Rein In the Pervasive Government Surveillance Enabled by Section 702'. American Civil Liberties Union. 11 April 2023. Accessed 22 December 2023. www.aclu.org/news/national-security/five-things-to-know-about-nsa-mass-surveillance-and-the-coming-fight-in-congress

Tegmark, Max. *Life 3.0: Being Human in the Age of Artificial Intelligence.* London: Penguin, 2017.

'The Brain Research through Advancing Innovative Neurotechnologies (BRAIN) Initiative: Revolutionising our Understanding of the Human

Brain'. National Institutes of Health: The BRAIN Initiative, no date. Accessed 25 December 2023. https://braininitiative.nih.gov/

'The Struggle to Create a Microchip that can Mimic the Human Brain and Open a Portal to Another World'. MindMaze, 20 June 2018. Accessed 25 December 2023. https://mindmaze.com/the-struggle-to-create-a-microchip-that-can-mimic-the-human-brain/

Thomas, Alexander. *The Politics and Ethics of Transhumanism: Techno-Human Evolution and Advanced Capitalism.* Bristol: Bristol University Press, 2024.

Tigard, Daniel W. 'Responsible AI and Moral Responsibility: A Common Appreciation'. *AI and Ethics.* Vol. 1, No. 2 (2020): pp. 113–117.

Tigard, Daniel W. 'There is No Techno-Responsibility Gap'. *Philosophy & Technology.* Vol. 34, No. 1 (2020): pp. 589–607.

'Toxic Twitter: How Twitter Generates Millions in Ad Revenue by Bringing Back Banned Accounts'. Center for Countering Digital Hate, 9 February 2023. Accessed 10 March 2023. https://counterhate.com/research/toxic-twitter/

'Transcript of Donald Trump's immigration speech'. *The New York Times.* 1 September 2016. Accessed 12 June 2024. www.nytimes.com/2016/09/02/us/politics/transcript-trump-immigration-speech.html

Turker, Habip. 'A Discussion of the Aesthetic Views of Ibn Sina and Aristotle on the Basis of Aesthetic Value'. In *Classic Issues in Islamic Philosophy and Theology Today*, edited by A-T. Tymieniecka and N. Muhtaroglu. Berlin: Springer, 2012: pp. 151–170.

Utrata, Alina. 'Lost in space'. *Boston Review.* 14 July 2021. Accessed 21 November 2023. www.bostonreview.net/articles/lost-in-space/

'UNESCO Promotes a Human-Rights Based Approach to AI Development during the Regional Forum on AI in Latin America and the Caribbean'. UNESCO. 17 December 2019. Accessed 18 December 2023. www.unesco.org/en/articles/unesco-promotes-human-rights-based-approach-ai-development-during-regional-forum-ai-latin-america

UNESCO. 'New UNESCO report warns that Generative AI threatens Holocaust memory'. *UNESCO.* 18 June 2024. Accessed 24 June 2024. www.unesco.org/en/articles/new-unesco-report-warns-generative-ai-threatens-holocaust-memory

United Nations. 'WHO guidance on Artificial Intelligence to improve healthcare, mitigate risks worldwide'. *UN News*, 28 June 2021. Accessed 12 July 2022. https://news.un.org/en/story/2021/06/1094902

US Department of Health & Human Services. 'The U.S. Public Health Service Untreated Syphilis Study at Tuskegee'. No date. Accessed 10

December 2024. www.cdc.gov/tuskegee/about/timeline.html?CDC_AAref_Val=https://www.cdc.gov/tuskegee/timeline.htm

Vaidhyanathan, Siva. 'Elon Musk's defense of Scott Adams shows why he is misguided and dangerous'. *The Guardian*. 1 March 2023. Accessed 12 April 2023. www.theguardian.com/commentisfree/2023/mar/01/elon-musks-defense-of-scott-adams-shows-why-he-is-misguided-and-dangerous.

Valdivia, Ana. 'Rural Spain could end up hosting infrastructure hubs for AI – here's what the environmental cost could be'. *The Conversation*. 21 June 2023. Accessed 12 December 2023. https://theconversation.com/rural-spain-could-end-up-hosting-infrastructure-hubs-for-ai-heres-what-the-environmental-cost-could-be-205504

Van Norden, Bryan W. *Taking Back Philosophy: A Multicultural Manifesto*. New York: Columbia University Press, 2017.

Véliz, Carissa. *Privacy is Power: Why and How You Should Take Back Control of Your Data*. London: Bantam, 2020.

Vergès, Françoise. *A Decolonial Feminism*, London: Pluto Press, 2021.

Virilio, Paul. *The Administration of Fear*. London: Semiotext(e), 2012.

Volkova, Svitlana, and Yoram Bachrach. 'On Predicting Sociodemographic Traits and Emotions from Communications in Social Networks and Their Implications to Online Self-Disclosure'. *Cyberpsychology, Behavior, and Social Networking*. Vol. 18, No. 12 (2015): pp. 726–736.

Wallach, Wendel, Stan Franklin, and Colin Allen. 'A Conceptual and Computational Model of Moral Decision Making in Human and Artificial Agents'. *Topics in Cognitive Science*. Vol. 2, No. 3 (2010): pp. 454–485.

Walzer, Richard. *Greek into Arabic: Essays on Islamic Philosophy*. Cambridge: Harvard University Press, 1962.

Wareham, Christopher S. 'Artificial Intelligence and African Conceptions of Personhood'. *Ethics and Information Technology*. Vol. 23, No. 2 (2021): pp. 127–136.

We Save the Mountain. 'Save The Mountain. No to the Lithium Mine'. Accessed 23 November 2023. https://en.goteo.org/project/salvemos-la-montana

Wesling, Meg. *Empire's Proxy: American Literature and U.S. Imperialism in the Philippines*. New York: New York University Press, 2011.

'What did Trump say? Explaining the former president's favourite talking points'. *NPR*. 11 May 2024. Accessed 12 June 2024. www.npr.org/2024/05/11/1245900177/trump-rally-speech-talking-points-rhetoric-immigration-abortion

White, Hayden. *Metahistory: The Historical Imagination in Nineteenth Century Europe*. Baltimore: Johns Hopkins Press, 1973.

'Why Are So Many Black Patients Dying of Skin Cancer?' Association of American Medical Colleges. 21 July 2022. Accessed 12 June 2024. www.aamc.org/news/why-are-so-many-black-patients-dying-skin-cancer

Wittig, Monique. *The Straight Mind and Other Essays*. Hemel Hempstead: Harvester Wheatsheaf, 1992.

Yang, Fan. 'A Glitch in Translation: (Self-)Orientalism and Post-Orientalism in Platform Governance'. Accessed 22 October 2023. https://law.yale.edu/sites/default/files/area/center/isp/documents/translation_ispessayseries_2023.pdf

Zuboff, Shoshana. *The Age of Surveillance Capitalism: The Fight for a Human Future at the New Frontier of Power*. London: Profile Books, 2019.

Index

1984 (Orwell) 1, 9

Aamer, Shaker 117
Abu Ghraib prison 107, 110, 111, 112, 113, 114, 117, 118
Adams, John 56
Adaptive Agent (AdA) 138
Adorno, Theodor 82
advisory boards 36–37
ageism 9, 10
AI for Children 37
AI-industrial complex 130, 138
Al-e Ahmad, Jalal 16
Algorithmic Justice League 16
algorithms
  bad algorithms 65, 67
  causal inferences 80–83
  improving algorithmic syntax for the future 81
  speed 80
  training data 9
  transversal algorithms 66–70
  'whitewashing' of 65
  see also bad data
al-Hallah, Mansur 45
al-ḥhikma philosophical tradition 25, 30–31

ALIZA 105
allgenugsam 41, 42, 43
Amazon 47, 65, 95–96
American Civil Liberties Union 64–65
Amnesty International 96
Anderson, Susan 26
anthropocentrism 127
anthropomorphisation 106
anti-Muslim bias 78, 94, 109–110, 114–115, 117
Arab Spring 77–78
archives 54, 59, 104, 133, 141
Argentina 3
Aristotle 28, 36, 139
art, digital 16, 139–140
Artificial General Intelligence (AGI) 38–39, 44, 68, 102–103
auditability 69, 97
avatars 6, 138
Azure Israel cloud region 95

bad data
  algorithmic illogic 9
  and bad algorithms 67
  causal inferences 81
  cod science 105

Index

bad data (*continued*)
  colonial histories 46, 58, 59
  in Europe and North America 23
  medical algorithms 62
  statistical literacy 85
  and untruth 103
Berkman Klein Center for Internet and Society 129
Beveridge, Albert 57, 58
biased datasets 9, 12–13, 22–24, 64–65
big data 5
Bilgin, Pinar 77
Bin Laden, Osama 94–95
biometric data 96
biopolitics 2, 59, 67, 127
biopower 2, 59, 116
Birhane, Abeba 15
Block, Ernst 139–140
Bonilla-Silva, Eduardo 60
brain-computer interfaces 41, 44, 66, 125–126
BRAIN initiative 127
Breivik, Anders 78, 94, 95
Buck v. Bell case 62
Buddhism 46
buen vivir 143
Buolamwini, Joy 16
Burgess, Joseph 33, 37, 38

capitalism 88, 89, 90
causal inferences 80–83, 131
Center for Countering Digital Hate 88
Centers for Disease Control and Administration 62
chatbots 10–11, 104, 105, 106
ChatGPT 13, 89, 102–103, 105

child abuse 13–14
China 28, 79, 91, 125–126, 143
CIA 105, 106–107, 111
clash regime 110
cleansed causal totalities 81
climate crisis 104–105, 141
coercion 95, 106–107, 111, 113, 134
cognitive science 125–126, 127
colonialism and coloniality
  civilising mission 45
  data colonialism 141
  expansionism 91
  forced sterilisation 63
  occupying Mars 90
  power 90
  resistance 118
  tech-giants 66
  'westtoxification' 16
  White heterosexual men 33, 53, 54, 55–56, 58–59, 61
common humanity 76–77, 116, 136–137
connectivity 140, 141, 142
consciousness 131, 138
counter-culture 16
creativity 79, 126, 127, 138, 139, 140
crime prevention 3
criminal liability 112–113
critical AI studies 15, 17, 54, 95, 134–135, 136
'culturally sensitive AI' 105, 110, 114, 115, 118
cyber attacks 6

Dabashi, Hamid 16
data centres 47, 142
de-centred perspectives 94
decolonialism 23, 27, 90, 118, 132, 138, 144

Index

DeepMind (Google) 126, 127, 138
dehumanisation 16, 96
Deleuze, Gilles 55
democracy 40, 78, 87–88, 133–135
Descartes, Rene 38
de-technologisation 128
dialect prejudice 104
Diaz, Owen 84, 85
difference, appreciation of 77
digital assistants 7, 12
dignity 95, 96, 134
disability discrimination 11
Doty, Roxanne Lynn 58

Eastern philosophy 25, 27, 30, 31, 37, 41, 76, 130
Eleuther AI 105
ELIZA 104–105, 106
emotions 14, 65, 105–106, 118, 131, 139, 141
empathy 37–38, 46, 85, 89, 92, 137
energy intensiveness 47, 142
Enlightenment, European
  and alienation from nature 47
  boundaries of thought 38
  causal inferences 81
  critical scholarship 46
  decolonising 144
  de-historicisation 80
  geopolitics 54–60
  imperialism 57, 90, 91
  and knowledge 45, 141
  language as a border-creating device 87
  ongoing legacy of 61, 67, 68
  philosophy 25, 26, 28, 30, 32, 33
  positivism 81–83
  racism 58, 59, 60
  religion 40
  social roles 130
  White heterosexual men 22–23
Enlightenment, Muslim 37–38
environmental issues 47, 141
ethical principles 25, 28
ethics manuals 46
eugenicism 11, 53–75, 86, 90, 91
Eurocentrism
  colonialism 53
  geopolitics 55
  globalisation 78
  versus hybrid knowledge 30–36
  identity politics 133
  international system 70
  philosophy 25, 29, 33–34, 37
exclusionary practices 30–36, 37, 93
extremism 67, 84, 87–88, 94, 95, 110, 129, 134

facial recognition software 3, 5, 9, 64–65, 96
fake art 139, 141
fake images 13
false categorisations 87
false information 88, 92, 93, 95
false narratives 85
Fanon, Frantz 23, 132
Farabi 35, 38, 39
Fay-Jones Report 112
fear 14–15
feminist scholarship 138
fight-or-flight 14–15
Foucault, Michel 2, 116
Frankfurt School 16
freedom 2–3, 42, 138
freedom of speech 88, 89
free will 40
fundamentalism 39, 45

Index

Galton, Francis 59
gamification 96
ganjis 28
Gates, Bill 12
Gaza 95–96
Generative Adversarial Network (GAN) 139
Geneva Convention 8, 109, 111, 115
geopolitics 54–60, 86, 90, 91, 141, 142
Gilroy, Paul 93
Global Forum on the Ethics of Artificial Intelligence 78
globalisation 78, 94, 140
Global South 33, 70
global thought 15, 26–29, 34, 36, 42, 45, 53–54, 129–131
global warming 47, 104, 142
God 38–39, 40, 41–45, 55, 57
Google 47, 95–96, 126, 138
governance 40
GPT-$_3$ and -$_4$ 103, 110
grand narratives 93
Greek philosophy 27, 28, 31, 32, 35, 36
Guantanamo Bay 113, 114, 115, 117

hacking 6
happy-cities 40, 44
healthcare 9, 141
Hegel, Georg Wilhelm Friedrich 37, 137
hegemony 36, 53, 70, 80, 128, 134
Heller, J.R. 64
Hitler, Adolf 9, 12, 13, 64
Hobson, John 70
homo-transphobia 23, 36
Horkheimer, Max 82

Hugging Face 47
human agency 2, 68, 138
humanistic approaches to AI 68, 89
humanities/arts 26–27, 69, 92, 119, 126, 127, 138–139
human-machine interface 40, 105, 106, 125–126, 127, 144
human rights 12, 14, 40, 69
Huntington, Samuel P. 87
hybridisation 6, 30–36, 70–71, 77, 93
hyper-capitalism 90, 143

Ibn Arabi 144
Ibn Khaldun 37–38
Ibn Rushd (Averroes) 27, 31–32, 33, 35, 40
Ibn Sina (Avicenna) 30, 31, 32, 38, 41, 42, 44, 139, 144
ideational systems 77–78
identity 47, 77, 86, 93, 131, 138
identity politics 34, 79, 93–94, 133, 134
ideology 31, 33–34, 53, 78, 86, 89, 91–92, 137
immigration 60, 78, 80, 86, 87, 95
imperialism 55–58, 66, 70, 78, 86, 89–97
implosions of AI 115–120
inclusivity 11, 78
Indigenous people 46, 62, 143
in-group/out-group 80, 87, 94, 95
see also 'other'
insurrection, human 139–145
intelligence agencies 109–110, 111–112

Index

Internet of Things (IoT) 13
interrogations 105, 107–109, 110–111, 113, 114, 117, 118
Israel 95

Jewish philosophers 32, 36
Jobin, Anna 28

Kant, Immanuel 30, 41, 42, 44–45, 46, 54
Khayyam, Omar 41–45
Kitaro, Nishida 46
Kurzweil, Raymond 40, 42
Kyong Chun, Wendy Hui 80
Kyoto School 46

LaMDA 136
language models 89, 103, 105, 109, 110
Latin America 3, 16, 68, 70, 90, 143
Laughlin, Harry 63
left-wing politics 70, 86
legal responsibility/liability 12, 112–113, 129
Lemoine, Blake 136
limitless expansion 91
local, the 8, 77, 78, 79, 93, 94
Locke, John 39, 46
LSD 107

machine ethics 24–48
machine gods 39–40
Maimonides 32, 35–36
Manichean allegories 83
maps of the world 90–91
Marcuse, Herbert 16
marginalised groups 33–34, 36, 58, 83, 86, 88, 104, 109, 132

marketing 5, 7, 83, 126, 128–129, 136
Mars, occupation of 86, 90, 91
medical algorithms 60–65
Melville, Herman 56
Mercator world map 90–91
Meta 142–143
Mexican border 3
microbial surveillance 4, 16, 46, 95, 141
microchipping 41, 44, 66
Microsoft 102–103
Mikolashek Report 107, 109
Miles, Steven 113
military-AI complex 125
mind control 67, 107, 118, 125
MindMaze 66
Minority Report 5
misinformation culture 88
misogyny 9, 23, 36, 87, 89, 110
MIT Media Lab 129
multiculturalism 34, 85
music 139–140, 143
Musk, Elon 12, 40, 66, 67, 84–89, 91, 134
mutual critique 46

nanotechnologies 66, 118
National Crime Agency (NCA) 13, 14
nature-human bonds 47
Nazi Germany 9, 12, 13, 64, 107
neighbourhood cyberwatches 97
neo-fascism 24, 67, 78, 84, 94
neo-Nazis 67, 78, 84, 87, 93, 94
networks of solidarity 97
Neuralink 39–40, 66
neuroethics 127

Index

neuroscience 125–126, 127
Nietzsche, Friedrich 38
non-human interfaces 47, 127
non-western perspectives 25–26, 27, 30–36, 37, 132, 143
Noriega, Maria 114
nuclear power 47

objectivity 81, 83, 92, 118, 130
off-grid living 128, 142
off-switch, lack of 106
'one-dimensional man' 16
OpenAI 102–3
Open Science Foundation 86
Orientalism 79, 86, 87, 89, 91, 110
origin stories 35, 41, 78
Orwell, George 1, 2, 9
Osei-Tutu, Kannin 69
'other' 31, 34, 59, 80, 82–83, 86, 94, 117, 128, 129, 137

Pachamama 47, 136
Paine, Thomas 56
Palestine 95–96
PaLM-E 138
panopticon 2, 3, 5
Parnet, Claire 55
patriarchy 92, 134
Pérez-Sales, Pau 115–116
perfectionism 11, 42
personal data 14, 109
Peru 29
philosophy
    centred philosophy versus universal ethics 30–36
    dei ex machina 36–47
    as master discipline 39
    Musk, Elon 92

    non-western perspectives 25–26, 27, 30–36, 37, 41, 76, 130, 132, 143
    as root discipline of global thought 26–28, 129–130, 131
    of science 24–48
Plato 28, 31, 32, 35, 36, 40
popular culture 143
population control 90
positivism 71, 81–83, 92, 103, 131
post-AI future 125–149
post-colonial theory 26, 90
posthumanism 7, 40, 80, 127, 136
posthuman warfare 7–8, 16, 46, 95
post-identity approaches 31
postmodernism 43, 77, 93
poststructuralism 26
power
    Asian 79
    biopower 2, 59, 116
    coloniality of power 90
    decolonisation of 144
    hierarchies of 86
    of holding secrets 83
    human supervision of AI's 128
    if-then propositions 80
    imperialism 78
    legitimisation by AI 134
    liquid formation of 4
    system 26
    tech utopias 93
    unidirectional 70
precariat 65
predicting future crimes 3
privacy 3, 14, 15, 68, 69, 95, 127–128, 140–142
Professorship in Global Thought and Comparative Philosophies 118

Index

profit-maximisation 8, 15, 84, 88–89, 129, 139, 141
Project MKUltra 107, 113
propaganda 12
pseudo-objectiveness 11–12
psychedelic drugs 107
psycho-codification 2, 4, 5, 16, 46, 55, 102–124, 140, 142
psychological intimidation tactics 106–107, 113, 115
Puerto Rico 62–63

Quijano, Aníbal 90, 118, 127, 130, 132

racism
  anti-Asian 79–80
  discrimination 9
  eugenic racism 53–75
  and free speech 89
  immigration 60
  imperialism 56–57
  interrogations 110–111
  language models 103–104
  medical algorithms 60–65
  non-western perspectives 34, 36
  as an ordering device 85
  Philippine-American War 58
  pschyo-nationalism 78
  racial filtering 65
  science 23, 32
  tech-giants 84–85
  terrorism 93
  Western philosophy 46
  White American narrative 57, 58–59
  against White people 85
reason and rationality 30, 31–32, 38, 81

recruitment of staff 10–11
regulation 142
reinforcement learning from human feedback (RLHF) 103
religion 38, 39, 40, 43–44, 83, 95
Renaissance 25
resistance 118, 143
resurrectionists 63
Rhodes, Cecil 92
'right to be left alone' 135, 137, 138
right-wing movements 12, 59–60, 67, 78, 84, 86–89, 128
robots 41, 66, 106, 135, 138
Russell, Bertrand 32

Said, Edward 87, 96
Salvemos la Montaña (We Save the Mountain) 143
scams 13
Schlesinger, James 111
science
  bad data 105
  counter-science 136
  critical science onto hard sciences 118, 137–138
  eugenicism 53–54
  future of scientific torture 102–124
  imperialism 90
  inevitabilities 92
  institutional harms and abuses 117–118, 133
  non-western perspectives 24–25, 35, 47
  philosophy of 24–48
  positivism 81–83
  social constructivism 134
  traditional Orientalism 87

Index

science (*continued*)
   and truth 129, 130
   value-laden 130
secularism 38, 41, 42, 45
sensory input 41, 60, 106
sentience 105, 136–137
Shah, Maitreva 11
Shariati, Ali 116
simplification 94
Sims, James Marion 61, 63
Singularity 40, 68, 103, 136
smart cities 3, 4–5, 6
social media 14, 24, 60, 78, 87, 88,
   94, 95, 140, 142
Sohravardi 31
Soros, George 86
souls 40
SpaceX 91
stereotypes 79, 104, 110
sterilisation 62–63
stress 14–15
Strickland, Lloyd 54
stupidity as asset on social
   media 94
surveillance 2–3, 4, 9, 60, 83,
   88–89, 95, 129, 137

taboos 114
Taguba, General Antonio M.
   110–111, 115
Tapia, Patricia 5
tech-giants 66–70, 83, 128–129
techno-colonialism 23
techno-fundamentalism 39, 45
techno-oppression 53
Techno-Orientalism 76–101, 110
techno-politics 1
Tegmark, Max 131
terrorism 8, 78–79, 93–94

Tesla 84, 85
Tianxia 143
Tigard, Daniel W. 28
Torre Centilena (Sentinel Tower) 3
torture 106–115, 116–117
totalitarianism 9, 94
transhumanism 39
transversal algorithms 66–70
Trump, Donald 59–60, 67, 86
truth
   conditions 35
   non-western perspectives 27
   post-AI future 129, 133
   rationalism 81
   search for supreme 31
   truth/lies boundary 9, 14, 22
   on X 88
Tuskegee study 64
Twain, Mark 56
Twitter (X) 86, 87, 88, 90–97

Uber 65
ubuntu 26, 144
UNESCO 12, 68, 131
UNICEF 37
United States 55–60, 63–65,
   131–132, 137
universal ethics versus centred
   philosophy 26–29
untruth 1, 22, 24, 69, 115

Véliz, Carissa 128
virtual friends 7
voice apps 13

Wang, Jia 54
Weizenbaum, Joseph 106
Wells, H.G. 90
Wesling, Meg 58

Index

'western' bias 71, 76, 79, 129
'westtoxicification' 16
White 23
White, Hayden 81
White heterosexual men 22–23, 33, 54, 55, 58–59, 61
White supremacism 23, 56, 58–59, 60, 87, 91

wisdom 28, 29, 32, 35
World Health Organization (WHO) 67–68

X *see* Twitter (X)

Zuboff, Shoshana 88
Zuckerberg, Mark 12

EU authorised representative for GPSR:
Easy Access System Europe, Mustamäe tee 50,
10621 Tallinn, Estonia
gpsr.requests@easproject.com

www.ingramcontent.com/pod-product-compliance
Lightning Source LLC
Chambersburg PA
CBHW011957150426
43200CB00018B/2930